How To Raise

Rabbits

For Fun and Profit

Milton I. Faivre

How To Raise
Rabbits
For Fun and Profit

Nelson-Hall Company

nh

Chicago

ISBN 0–911012–47–8

Library of Congress Catalog Card No. 73–81277

Manufactured in the United States of America

To Dave

whose youthful interest in rabbit
raising gave birth to this book.

Contents

Illustrations

How To Raise

Rabbits

For Fun and Profit

Preface

How to Raise Rabbits for Fun and Profit is not intended to be a technical book on genetics nor is it written to appeal to the managers of large commercial rabbitries, whose requirements and experiences are in a class by themselves. It is geared, rather, to the beginner, who may be confused by conflicting views and instructions found in magazines, by fancy advertisements, and by the advice of other rabbit fanciers.

Admittedly, there is very little that is new in the how-to-do-it of rabbit raising. However, many of the basic details that the newcomer must know are left out of printed material either through oversight or because the authors feel that the information is too elementary to be included. Here these basic details are covered since I believe no fact is too elementary to the novice.

This book attempts to act as a starting point and a guide whereby the beginner can learn, step by step, the fundamentals required for success. Once the rabbitry is on its way, the newcomer should branch out, leaving this book and going on to more technical ones, some of which are listed in the bibliography.

For some time I have owned a large rabbitry, and have tried to help those who asked me for assistance. The material in this book is a combination of answers to questions asked and information I was forced to find out or to learn the hard way because it wasn't included in already-published reference material.

While I accept full responsibility for the content of this book, I want to thank those who contributed material and who helped in one way or another. I would like particularly to express my appreciation to the United States Department of Agriculture for their willingness to answer questions and to provide the requested material. Among those who assisted in the USDA, Miss Mary Cowen of the Film Library was especially helpful in locating many of the photos. Without her willingness to search for photos, this book would be of little value.

The secretaries of many rabbit specialty clubs were also very helpful, allowing me to use much of their material in order to correctly describe particular breeds. Thanks also to Mr. Willis Tate, Gulf Comprehensive High School, New Port Richey, Florida; to Mrs. Janet Lewis, Librarian, New Port Richey Public Library; to Hobby's Rabbitry, Tampa, Florida; and to the many rabbit fanciers who offered advice.

The material in this book will start the reader in the right direction, but the success of any rabbitry depends on commitment.

Introduction

Welcome to the fascinating and profitable world of the domestic rabbit. Whether your interest is to keep a rabbit for a pet, to raise a few for exhibit in shows across the country, or to have a small backyard rabbitry that will provide meat for the table, the domestic rabbit will meet your requirements.

Rabbit raising is delightful and interesting. It is ideally suited to city areas or to small farms of just a few acres. Both the 4-H and FFA organizations include it in their programs, and the Boy Scouts and Girl Scouts issue merit badges to those who successfully raise a litter of rabbits. As pets, rabbits are ideal; they make no noise, require little living area, eat kitchen scraps, and their manure may be used for garden fertilizer.

Introduction

A grand champion rabbit and trophy being proudly displayed by a youthful rabbit raiser. Rabbits are an excellent project for all youth groups.

A backyard rabbitry with four does and a buck will provide a steady supply of high protein, all-white meat for the table. According to the United States Department of Agriculture, more than fifty million pounds of rabbit meat are consumed by Americans in an average year. This meat is raised in small backyard rabbitries as well as on large commercial farms.

An increasing demand for rabbits for laboratory and biological purposes offers opportunities to breeders living near medical schools, hospitals, and laboratories. Rabbits have been used for research in venereal disease, cardiac surgery, hypertension, and virology, and are important tools in infectious disease research, toxin and antitoxin development, and anatomy and physiology instruction. A recent development in the rabbit industry has been the increased use by scientific personnel of various rabbit organs and tissues in specialized research.

Rabbit skins have commercial value. The better grades may be dressed, dyed, sheared, and made into garments or used for trimmings. Some skins are used for slipper and glove linings, for toys, and in making felt. Fine shreds of the flesh part of the dried skins, left after separating the fur in making felt, are used for making glue. Because of the relatively low value of skins from meat rabbits, a large volume is necessary to market them satisfactorily.

Once you have made the decision to raise rabbits, there will be many questions to answer for yourself. First of all, why do you want to raise rabbits? Is it for meat? For show? Or just to have a nice quiet pet or two around the house? If you decide to raise them for meat, you must find out if there is a local market for your supply. Also, find out what breed would be best for your meat customers.

Suppose you decide to raise rabbits primarily for show. Is there a rabbit club in your neighborhood? If not, are there other rabbit fanciers living near you who show their rabbits and who would be willing to assist you?

You'll have scores of questions to answer as you begin your new hobby. This book will answer the majority of them. And don't be afraid to ask questions of other rabbitmen, your feed dealer, or the American Rabbit Breeders Association, 4323 Murray Avenue, Pittsburgh, Pennsylvania 15217. The ARBA is an organization of rabbitmen, both youths and adults, who are ready and willing to help the newcomer start off on the right track.

Before we begin the how-to of rabbit raising, a word of warning. There is no quick way to make money in the rabbit business. You must first study your animals, learn their habits, and get experience in all phases of the hobby before any profit will materialize. Don't believe the ads that promise fantastic profits in a short time. The only one making money from those ads is the guy who sells the information. Common sense will tell you that it's impractical to raise, house, and feed rabbits, and then ship them cross-country by freight to a dealer and expect to make a dime. Nobody has and nobody will. The ARBA is constantly fighting these fraudulent ads.

Now, let's look at a few of the many breeds of rabbits.

one
Rabbit Breeds

Your choice of a breed of rabbit to raise will be determined largely by your reason for raising rabbits—whether they are to be raised for fur, show, or meat. As a beginner, you will quite likely be confused by the more than thirty recognized breeds and even more color varieties that are listed by the American Rabbit Breeders Association. This chapter is designed to help you make the decision by describing some of the breeds in detail plus acquainting you with their actual appearance by means of photos.

Make your decision wisely, since your choice will require patience, attention, considerable work, and, yes, even love. Visit other rabbitries, subscribe to the various rabbit magazines, join the ARBA, check with local Future Farmers of America (FFA) chapters, and contact area 4-H Clubs. Both of these youth-based groups welcome adults who wish to look in on their activities. Be inquisitive, ask questions no matter how elementary you feel they may be, and then determine what breed catches your fancy and imagination the most.

The following breeds have proven to be the most popular across the country, and breeding stock is more readily obtainable for these particular breeds than for others. There is a more complete listing of breeds and color varieties at the end of this chapter.

Californian

This is a large white rabbit with black ears, feet, nose, and tail. At maturity it will weigh between 8 and 10 1/2 pounds. The Californian began its development in 1923 when crosses between the Himalayan and Chinchilla produced an excellent buck with good fur and meat qualities. This buck was then mated to a New Zealand doe. In 1928, the first rabbit of the type now called Californian was developed. This breed is very popular among both small fanciers and large commercial rabbitries as a meat rabbit.

Champagne d'Argent

This is one of the oldest breeds and has been raised successfully in France for more than a hundred years. It is well known as a commercial breed. The fur is useful in its natural state, and is still one of the leading furs used in the manufacture of clothes in Europe.

At birth the rabbit is black; at about three or four months of age, it takes on the adult color, which is silver or a skimmed-milk color with a dark slate-blue undercoat. Ideal weight for bucks is 10 pounds, for does, 10 1/2 pounds. It is also known as the French Silver.

New Zealand

Although named New Zealand, this rabbit is completely American in origin. Its ancestors were the Belgian Hare and the Golden Fawn, both very popular before the New Zealand came along. The New Zealand breed may be divided into three distinct categories: New Zealand Red, New Zealand Black, and New Zealand White. This is the most widely raised breed in the country today.

Although all three types are excellent meat rabbits, the New Zealand White fur is in greatest demand by garment makers because it takes a variety of dyes successfully. Also, of all the

A Californian Rabbit

The New Zealand White Rabbit

The Flemish Giant Rabbit

A Siamese Satin Grand Champion

breeds, the New Zealand is most in demand as a laboratory animal.

Chinchilla

There are three varieties of Chinchilla rabbits being raised today: the Giant, the American, and the Standard. All three have excellent qualities. The American Chinchilla in particular is highly prized for its gray surface fur, deep blue-gray underfur, and white belly. The American Chinchilla buck weighs 10 pounds at maturity and the doe weighs 11 pounds.

Flemish Giant

The Flemish Giant is the largest breed of rabbit being raised today. Some bucks have been known to reach 22 pounds at maturity. Their color is varied, appearing as steel gray, light gray, white, blue, sandy, fawn, or black. This is an excellent show rabbit, and the varying fur colors make it a challenge to raise. Ideal mature weight is over 13 pounds.

Dutch

This rabbit had its origin in Holland, coming into England in 1864. Of all the rabbits raised primarily for show, the Dutch is by far the most popular. This rabbit may be recognized by the white band over the shoulders, under the neck, and over the front legs and hind feet. The remainder of the rabbit may be gray, chocolate, blue, black, tortoise, or steel gray. This coloration has been found to be genetically determined, making the Dutch ideal for the breeder who likes variety. Ideal weight ranges from 3 1/2 to 5 1/2 pounds.

Siamese Satin

This is another all-American breed, having a soft, silky texture to its fur, together with a brilliant luster. The markings are similar to those of a Siamese cat. The Siamese Satin makes a fine show animal and the pelt is in wide demand because of its texture and unusual coloring. Ideal weight varies from 8 to 11 pounds. Others in the Satin family are the Black, Red, Blue, and White. All are excellent meat animals also.

Himalayan

The Himalayan closely resembles the Californian, although it is much smaller in size. It weighs at maturity from 2 1/2 to 5 pounds. The body fur is white, very short, fine, soft, and pure in color. The colored markings on the ears, nose, and feet are velvety in texture.

Polish

A very popular show animal commonly nicknamed "The Little Aristocrat," the Polish has very tiny ears and bold eyes. The fur may be chocolate, white, or black. Brown eyes are found in either the black or chocolate Polish, ruby or blue eyes in the white variation. Ideal weight is 2 1/2 pounds.

Checkered Giant

The Checkered Giant has a German origin and at one time was known as the German Checkered Giant. White predominates on this animal, with markings of black or blue. Due to its unusual markings, the Checkered is in demand both as a show and a fur animal. It is also an excellent meat animal. Ideal weight for the Checkered Giant is in the 12 to 14 pound range.

Angora

The Angora is the only rabbit not being raised for its pelt; rather, its soft, high-strength wool is its product. The breeder can keep his Angora rabbits indefinitely, without having to sell or slaughter them.

Each mature Angora will produce an

16

average of 14 to 16 ounces of wool a year. The wool grows at a remarkable rate, approximately an inch a month. It is removed by shearing, which does not harm the animal.

The Angora is an excellent show rabbit, has good meat, and as mentioned above its wool is valuable. Ideal weight is 5 to 8 pounds, and there are four basic color varieties: white, fawn, blue, and black.

Before you decide to raise Angoras for their wool alone, determine the market. Many processors will take only large quantities of wool, and it must be graded before shipment.

Belgian Hare

The Belgian Hare was really the first show rabbit in America. As its name implies, it is of Belgian origin. Unlike other breeds, it assumes a stand-up position. This, together with its graceful body and alert expression, makes it a favorite of many of the old-time fanciers. This rabbit is found in three color varieties: red, tan, and chestnut. Its ideal weight is 8 pounds.

courtesy Francis P. F

The Himalayan

The Checkered Giant Rabbit

18

The Angora

The Belgian Hare

Rabbit Breeds and Varieties

Breed	Weight	Color	Use
American	8-11 lb.	blue and white	meat, fur, show
American Silver Fox	8-12 lb.	black and blue	meat, fur, show
Angora Wooler	5 lb. and up	black, blue, fawn, white	wool, show
Belgian Hare	8 lb.	red, tan, chestnut	show
Beveren	7½ lb. and up	blue, white, blue-eyed black	show
Californian	8-10½ lb.	white with colored nose, ears, feet, and tail	meat, show
Champagne d'Argent	9-12 lb.	white, silver, blue undercoat	show, meat
Checkered Giant	11 lb. and up	white and black or blue	show, fur, meat
Chinchilla	9-12 lb.	gray with white belly	show, fur
Dutch	3½-5½ lb.	white and black, blue, chocolate, tortoise, gray, or steel gray	show, laboratory
English Spot	9-12 lb.	white with black, blue, chocolate, tortoise, lilac, gray, or steel-gray spots	show, meat, laboratory

Rabbit Breeds

Breed	Weight	Color	Use
Flemish Giant	13 lb. and up	black, steel gray, light gray, sandy, blue, white, or fawn	show, meat
Havana	5-7 lb.	chocolate, blue	fur, show
Himalayan	2½-5 lb.	white with colored nose, ears, feet, and tail	show, laboratory
Lilac	5½-9 lb.	pinkish gray	fur, meat, show
Lops	10 lb. and up	gray	show
Marten	5-9½ lb.	chocolate, silver, silver sable, black, blue	fur, show
New Zealand	9-12 lb.	red, white, black	meat, show
Palomino	9-11 lb.	golden, lynx	meat, show
Polish	2½-3½ lb.	white, black, chocolate	show, laboratory
Rex	7 lb. and up	numerous colors	show, fur
Satin	8-11 lb.	black, red, blue, copper, white	meat, show, fur
Silver	6 lb.	gray, fawn, chocolate	show
Tan	4-6 lb.	black and tan, blue and tan	show

Note: For a complete list of all breeds and varieties, contact the American Rabbit Breeders Association.

21

two
Selection of Stock

The selection of a breed is often a matter of personal preference after the general purpose (meat, show, fur, or laboratory) has been determined. For the beginner, selecting healthy breeding stock is more important than knowing the fine points of difference between breeds. If the objective of the rabbitry is production of meat, then the use of one of the heavy or medium weight breeds would be logical. For this, the New Zealand or the Californian would be ideal. Pelts from white rabbits bring a higher price than pelts from colored rabbits, so the selection of a white breed has an advantage in terms of selling the pelts after slaughtering for meat.

Once the breed has been chosen, the

selection of animals that are of good quality and type, and free from disease, is very important. Animals that are healthy and vigorous—as evidenced by proper weight for age and breed, smooth hair coat, bright eyes, and alertness— should be chosen.

The beginning rabbit fancier may start with young rabbits just weaned or with mature animals. There are advantages to either way of beginning.

When young rabbits are used to begin a rabbitry, the breeder has a chance to become acquainted with his stock and their habits before they reach the age to breed. As I mentioned in the Introduction, it is always best to begin with one buck and a few does, and expand the rabbitry as more experience is gained and a market is developed.

When you select stock to begin your rabbitry, you should keep several points in mind in order to make the best possible selection. The following ten points will serve as an excellent guide.

1. Select local stock that can be inspected so you can see what you are purchasing. Also, you will have a chance to ask questions.

2. Purchase stock only from reliable breeders who have records on the litters, weight, and diseases of their stock.

3. Always select stock from families that

have a history of heavy milk production.

4. Select from families that produce large litters.

5. Select stock that is free from undesirable characteristics, such as malocclusion or woolies.

6. Select from families with a history of long life. This allows maximum return from the breeding dollar.

7. Always purchase stock that show a definite resistance to disease.

8. Select does with a family history of producing at least four litters a year.

9. Select from families that show fast, steady growth.

10. Select from families that show good type. This means that no matter what breed you select, it should meet the requirements for that breed as outlined by the ARBA.

The price tag on a rabbit is no indication of its actual worth. Only the animal's record gives you the information necessary to determine its value as a breeding animal.

Breeders who neglect to keep records, or rabbitries that offer excess animals for sale without any specific information regarding their background, may be honest and may even provide at times the type of breeding stock you desire, but you are risking the future of your rabbitry if you buy such rabbits.

If you are not acquainted with a good

breeder, contact your agricultural agent, the various feed stores in your area, and of course the ARBA. From these sources at least one reputable breeder should be located. If you are sure of your source of supply for good breeding stock, you may be sure of the future of your own rabbitry.

Although excellent breeding stock may be purchased by mail, the beginner is advised to buy locally at first; then not only does he see what he is buying, but he has a chance to talk to the breeder. The information he gets this way will be valuable as he begins to develop his rabbitry. Also, all good breeders guarantee their stock, so if something happens when you first place the new animal in your rabbitry, you have a chance to return it to the breeder. I have found this to be very important with my own rabbitry, as on occasion stock that has been purchased has developed disease even though all the selection points had been followed exactly.

Selection of Fryer Stock

In addition to the ten general selection points, the beginning rabbit raiser should consider the following five points when selecting breeding stock to be used primarily for fryers.

1. *Size of litter.* Maximum profits are obtained from litters that contain large, well-

developed young. A profitable doe should regularly kindle seven to ten young at least four times a year. With proper care and adequate records, a fifth litter can be obtained.

2. *Milk production.* Heavy milk production by the nursing doe is extremely important. Rapid growth of young rabbits, which insures maximum profit when they are sold, is directly related to the amount of milk produced by the doe. The weight of the litter at the end of three weeks will serve as a definite indication of the milk supply. If the weight of an individual baby rabbit is less than 3/4 pound or if the litter weighs less than 5 1/2 pounds, the doe is not providing sufficient milk and should be replaced. Remember, I am talking about fryer litters only.

3. *Correct type.* Some breeds of rabbit are suitable for meat production while others are not. If you are raising rabbits primarily for meat, it is important that they weigh 4 pounds at eight weeks of age. The smaller breeds are unsuitable to be used as fryers for commercial production. They are, however, acceptable for home consumption.

4. *Regular reproduction.* When does miss in their summer matings and during molting in the fall, they have fewer litters, resulting in less income for the rabbitry. If a doe can produce five litters a year, she is a profitable animal and

is giving a good return on the investment dollar. This is true for the small backyard rabbitry and for the large commercial venture.

5. *Longevity and resistance to disease.* A rabbitry that experiences high rates of sickness and death will not be able to show the necessary profit margin. Even the small backyard rabbitry cannot be successful if the rabbit fancier is forced to replace his animals frequently. The initial higher cost of a good grade of rabbit will be more than offset by better litters, less disease, and more contented rabbits. There is no such thing as a contented sick animal.

The selection of good stock, whether for show, pets, or meat, is very important. Take the time to find the best animals; then treat them with respect and they will repay you many times over.

three
Housing and Equipment

The first step in building a rabbitry, even before purchasing a particular breed of rabbit, is providing suitable housing for the animals. Without proper housing, all your efforts will be in vain.

Many newcomers to the rabbit world do not realize that some communities and housing developments specifically forbid the raising of any animals. Therefore, before you spend money on rabbits or equipment, find out whether you will be allowed to keep them.

With the present rapid population growth being experienced in many sections of the country, areas which at one time had no zoning restrictions now have very strict laws. Also, in some areas there are health department

29

requirements that must be met. If you are unsure of local regulations, investigate. Then you
will not spend considerable time and money
only to find that no rabbits are allowed.

BUILDINGS

The type of building you will need for
housing the hutches will be determined by local
building regulations, climatic conditions, your
plans for the rabbitry, and the amount of money
available to invest in the project. When you plan
your building and its equipment, emphasize the
comfort of the animals and the ease of taking
care of them. If your housing is hard to take care
of, or unsuitable for local conditions, you are
beaten before you begin. A rabbitry should be
an enjoyment.

The building should have a simple design,
protect the rabbits from the wind, rain, and
bright sun, and provide light and fresh air. If
your area has a mild climate, hutches may be
placed in the open, but they should have individual roofs and protection for the rabbits from
occasional bad weather.

Sunlight aids in maintaining a sanitary condition in the rabbitry, but whether it actually
helps the rabbits themselves has not been determined. Rabbits apparently enjoy being in the
sun when the temperature is low or moderate,

but exposure to direct hot sunlight may have a serious effect on them. I have observed in my own rabbitry that rabbits prefer the shaded areas of their cages during the hot summer days.

Although all rabbits suffer from extremely high temperatures, newborn litters and does well advanced in pregnancy suffer the most. Restlessness in the young and rapid breathing and excessive moisture around the mouth of the doe are sure signs of overheating.

In mild climates, hutches may be placed in the shade of trees or buildings, or in a simple open shed with just a roof for protection from weather.

In hot climates, some cooling system must be provided in addition to the available shade. Cooling can be accomplished by the use of overhead sprinklers or foggers placed within the building. Make sure that the building is adequately ventilated and that the rabbits receive the benefit of any prevailing breezes. In areas where strong winds and stormy weather prevail, put the hutches in a building that is open to the south and east; use curtains or panels to close up the building during inclement weather. Where the weather is extremely cold, more protection will be needed.

When you plan housing for your rabbit herd, remember that they should be protected from getting wet. Proper housing should

31

Semienclosed hutches such as these may be used in climates where continual cold weather is a problem.

provide a dry, ventilated home for your rabbits. Damp, matted fur not only is unsightly but promotes disease. If a rabbit should get wet, take a dry, soft towel and rub its fur. A firm but gentle motion will accomplish the job in a few moments, and will restore the fur to its proper appearance. Never use a hair dryer on your rabbit.

HUTCHES

Mature rabbits are housed individually and should have 1 square foot of floor space for each pound of body weight. This means that an 8-pound rabbit should have a hutch with a floor that has 8 square feet of surface area.

Hutches should be no more than 2 1/2 feet deep so you can easily reach the rabbits to take care of them. Height should be from 18 to 24 inches. Make the hutches 3 feet long for small breeds, 3 or 4 feet long for the medium sized breeds, and 4 to 6 feet long for the giant breeds. (All figures given are for inside measurements.)

Whether you arrange the hutches on one level or in two or three tiers depends on how much room you have available. Waist-high hutches are preferable as they are the most convenient for observing the rabbits and will save you time and labor when feeding and removing the waste matter. Arranging hutches in two or three tiers, which is necessary where space is at a premium, is not entirely satisfactory. It is difficult to care for and to observe the rabbits in the bottom and top tiers. Squatting or stooping to feed and care for the rabbits in the bottom tier, and climbing a stool or ladder for the top row of a three-tier arrangement, results in additional labor and time spent.

Rabbits are more easily cared for in well-built hutches than in poorly constructed, temporary ones. It takes just as long to build a temporary cage as it does a permanent one. Why do double work?

All - Wire Cages

Self-cleaning, all-wire hutches need no bedding and can easily be kept in good condition. Sanitation becomes a very minor problem and there will be no need for repair due to chewing.

courtesy USDA

The all-wire Quonset-hut-shaped cage is clean, economical, and easy to take care of. Notice the feed hoppers made from 5-gallon cans and the nest boxes under the cages.

34

Several different models are available commercially or you can easily build one yourself. Plans and specifications may be obtained from a number of commercial firms that advertise regularly in all the rabbit magazines.

An all-wire Quonset-hut-shaped hutch has several advantages. It is easy to clean, neat in appearance, and requires less wire than does a standard rectangular hutch. The hutch features a door that opens over the top. When open, the door does not occupy aisle space nor interfere with feeding and cleaning operations. In addition, when this type of hutch is placed at waist height, you can reach all the corners without putting your head and shoulders inside the door opening.

Quonset-hut-shaped hutches can be adapted to fit any type of rabbitry where hutches are protected. They are most easily constructed in units, two hutches per unit.

Material for Two Quonset-Hut-Shaped Hutches in One Unit

The following material will be needed to build one unit containing two hutches. Each hutch will be 3 feet long and 2 1/2 feet wide.
Floor:

One piece of welded, 16 gauge galvanized wire, 1- by 1/2-inch mesh, 3 feet wide by 6 feet long.

35

Top:

One piece of welded, 14 gauge galvanized wire, 1- by 2-inch mesh, 4 feet wide by 6 feet long.

Ends and Partition:

Three pieces of welded, 14 gauge galvanized wire, 1- by 2-inch mesh, 1 1/2 feet wide by 2 1/2 feet long.

Doors:

Two pieces of welded, 14 gauge galvanized wire, 1- by 2-inch mesh, 1 1/2 feet wide by 1 foot 8 inches long.

Miscellaneous:

Steel rod: 5/16 inch round steel rod, 8 feet 11 inches.

Two pieces, 2 feet 6 1/2 inches long for nest supports.

One piece, 3 feet 10 inches long, for reinforcing the front of the hutch.

Wire: No. 12 galvanized, 21 feet 7 1/2 inches.

Three pieces, 4 feet long, for edging around ends and partition.

Two pieces, 9 1/4 inches long, for vertical nest support.

Two pieces, 1 foot 4 1/4 inches long, for horizontal nest support.

Two pieces, 2 feet long, for feeder yokes.

Wire: No. 9 galvanized, 7 feet 4 inches.

Two pieces, 1 foot 8 inches long, for additional support at the ends of the hutch.

Two pieces, 2 feet long, for reinforcing the door openings.

Fasteners:

100 hen-cage clips, small size, for fastening the floor, top ends, and partition.

25 hen-cage clips, large size, for door hinges and for fastening the No. 9 wire.

30 hog rings, No. 101, for fastening the 5/16 inch steel rod to the floor.

Door latches: Any standard latch or fastener may be used.

In the construction of a unit of two hutches, it is recommended that the floor be laid out first, 3 inches to be bent up on either side (the front and rear of the hutches), and openings cut for the nest boxes. The 3-inch margin can be bent up on the sides with a metal brake or some kind of improvised homemade tool. When you cut openings for the nest boxes be sure to leave approximately 1 1/2 inches of flooring at the front of the hutch for suspension of the boxes.

The partition and ends should then be shaped from 1-inch by 2-inch wire by using a template. Allow 5/8 inch protrusion beyond the edge of the template and bend these wires around the No. 12 edging wire. At this time, some No. 12 wire may be fastened to the bottom of the ends and partitions for reinforcement. The ends and partitions can then be laid in position on the floor and fastened to the floor with hen-cage clips.

Next, make the top from 1-inch by 2-inch wire, cutting openings for the doors and feeders. Lay the top over the floor, ends, and partitions, and fasten it at the rear with hen-cage clips spaced approximately every 5 inches. Raise the front edge of the top until it is even with the 3-inch raised front edge of the flooring and fasten with hen-cage clips. Now, reach in one end and raise the other end enclosure into position, fastening it to the top with hen-cage clips. Repeat this process with the center partition and other end enclosure. This will automatically form the Quonset-hut-shape top over the ends and partition. The raised front edge can then be cut for installation of the feeders, the doors and nest boxes can be installed, and the hutch is ready for use.

When two or more units (four or more hutches) are built and placed end to end, a saving of one end enclosure can be made for each unit by using the following procedure:

1. Cut the wire mesh for the floor and top of the first unit 6 feet, 1 inch long.

2. On the first unit, fasten the partition 3 feet from the left end enclosure and fasten the right end enclosure 3 feet to the right of the partition. This will leave a 1-inch overhang to connect to the next unit.

3. On all additional units, cut the floor and top wire 6 feet long and fasten the partition 35 inches from the left end; fasten the right end enclosure 3 feet to the right of the partition, leaving 1 inch of floor and top extending beyond the right-end enclosure. These end enclosures become partitions when units are added.

4. Use hen-cage clips to fasten the units into one continuous line.

These hutches can be installed in several ways. Suspension from the rafters or ceiling of a shed is the most practical method because it eliminates all supports beneath the hutches. Heavy wire or light lumber can be used to hang the hutches. If a dewdrop water system is used in the rabbitry, the hutches can be fastened to the water pipe for rear support. If a plastic pipe is used, do not fasten the hutch to it. If the hutches are not placed within a shed, they can be supported by a frame on legs. Some type of cover will be necessary, however, to protect the rabbits from the rain, sun, and wind.

There are other all-wire cages that may be built, but the Quonset-hut-type will be the easiest for the beginner.

Wooden-Frame Wire Hutches

Though not so durable as the all-wire hutch, the wooden hutch with woven wire sides and ends permits good circulation of air. It is also more sanitary than the all-wood hutch. Hutches may be supported in several ways. If you use corner posts, make them long enough so that you can clean underneath the hutches and do other work around them. A hutch can also be rested on crosspieces nailed between the studs that support the shed, or you can hang the hutch from the rafters or ceiling of the shed with heavy wire or light lumber.

Semienclosed Hutches

The semienclosed hutch is constructed with ends and back made of wood. An extended roof gives added protection. You can use this type of hutch in outdoor rabbitries in cold climates.

Another satisfactory type of hutch, which is light, movable, and inexpensive, is one made with a wire back, wire sides, and a wire floor, but with a solid roof. The solid roof allows the hutch to be used outdoors without having to provide another shelter to place it in.

Hutch Floors

Several types of floor are used in hutches, and each has its own particular merit. Wire mesh floors are used extensively where a self-cleaning type is desired. This is a necessity in commercial herds, where it would be impossible to secure enough help to keep solid floors in a topnotch sanitary condition.

When you are installing this type of floor, examine the wire for sharp points, which result sometimes from the galvanizing process. Always put the smooth surface on the top. Solid floors should slope slightly to the rear to provide proper drainage. You can use hardwood slats, 1 inch wide, and spaced 5/8 or 3/4 inch apart. A combination of solid floor at the front part of the hutch and slats or a strip of mesh wire at the back may be used.

FEEDING EQUIPMENT

It is desirable as well as convenient to use crocks, troughs, hoppers, and hay managers that are large enough to hold several feedings. Use a type that will prevent waste and contamination of feed.

Crocks

Crocks specially designed for rabbit feeding are not easily tipped over and have a lip that prevents the animals from scratching out and wasting their feed. The chief objection to these is that the young rabbits get into them and contaminate the feed.

courtesy USDA

This type of all-wire cage contains a hay manger on the left, a cooling basket for the young in hot weather, a nail-keg nest box, and a water crock for easy watering.

Hay Mangers and Troughs

Hay mangers with troughs to prevent wastage may be incorporated into hutches if hay or green feeds form a part of the diet. The troughs also may be used for supplemental grains or home-grown feeds. Troughs may be constructed so that they can be pulled out of the hutch for cleaning, filling, and disinfecting. Guards placed on the feed troughs and spaced just far enough apart to allow mature animals to feed will help keep the young rabbits out of the troughs and the feed.

Hoppers

Feed hoppers of the proper design and size save considerable time and labor. These can be constructed from metal, wood, Masonite, or other readily available material. They should hold enough food for several days and be placed within the hutch or suspended on the outside. The opening through which the rabbits obtain feed should be no more than 4 inches above the hutch floor so that the young rabbits can readily obtain food.

An inexpensive feed hopper that will hold about 15 pounds of pellets or grain can be made from a square 5-gallon can. First, cut off the top. Then cut two holes opposite each other in the sides. (If the hopper is to be hung on the side of the hutch, cut a hole in one side only.) The holes should be 4 inches high, 4 inches from the bottom, and 1 inch from each side. Bend the rough edges inward to give a smooth edge and to add rigidity. Take a 1-inch by 4-inch by 13 1/2-inch board and cut it diagonally into two equal triangular pieces. Use these as supports for the baffle boards, which are nailed to them.

The baffle boards, of 1/2-inch plywood,

should extend 1 inch below the bottom of the side openings of the can. The space between the lower ends of the baffle boards permits the grain or pellets to flow down as the rabbits eat. Make the baffle boards fit snugly against the sides of the can so feed cannot slip by. Mount the top corners of the baffles so that each baffle will rest against the top edge of the can.

Cover the exposed edges of boards with tin to prevent gnawing. Put a finishing nail in the outer edge of the triangular piece supporting the baffle, and bend the nail to hook over the lower lip of the opening to hold it and the baffle in place.

You can save hutch floor space by using a hopper with a feed opening on one side only and setting it part way into the hutch. Cut an opening large enough to accommodate the hopper in the side of the hutch. Then wire the top of the hopper to the hutch for support. One short baffle on the side opposite the hopper opening will keep feed out of the rear corners.

A single-compartment feed hopper is used when only one kind of feed is given. When mixed feed that the rabbits can separate is offered, the feed will be selectively consumed. The rabbits scratch out and waste the part they prefer not to eat. You can prevent this waste by using a hopper that has individual compartments for each feed.

EQUIPMENT FOR WATERING

Rabbits should have clean, fresh water at all times.

Crocks

Half-gallon water crocks are still used extensively. Fasten them in the hutches so that the rabbits will not tip them over. If part of the crock extends through the front wall of the hutch, refill the crock without opening the hutch door. Clean and disinfect the crocks periodically.

Coffee Cans

Coffee cans are especially useful for watering rabbits during cold weather because you can easily break the ice and remove it. Cans are, however, easily tipped over unless they are fastened to a board.

Automatic Watering Systems

Automatic watering systems are widely used in commercial rabbitries, and are better than water crocks and coffee cans. They eliminate the tedious and time-consuming chores of washing, disinfecting, rinsing, and filling. They supply fresh, clean water for the rabbits at all times. When an automatic watering system is properly installed, dirt and fur will not collect in it and plug it up.

In cold climates, an automatic watering system must be protected against winter freezing unless the hutches are in a heated enclosure. Protection may be obtained through the use of heating cables wrapped around, or running through, the water pipe. If winter temperatures are not too severe, protection against freezing can be obtained by having valves at the ends of the water lines and allowing water to dribble through the pipes during short periods of subfreezing temperatures.

If you can cut and thread pipe, you can install an automatic watering system. With the advent of plastic pipes, the project has become much easier. Conventional systems sold by rabbit and poultry supply houses consist of a pressure-reducing tank equipped with a float valve, a 1/2-inch supply pipe, a watering unit for each hutch, and valves. The valves are used to bleed out air bubbles, to drain the system as needed, or to shut off the water.

If the water contains sediment, a half-barrel can be used in place of the standard pressure-reducing tank. The outlet for the supply pipe is installed several inches above the bottom of the barrel. The sediment will then collect below the outlet pipe and will not get into the system and clog it. Other sediment traps installed between the tank and the supply pipe to the hutches can be used with any type of tank.

One-gallon or smaller tanks sometimes are used where the weather is warm. Such tanks are emptied more often. The continual flow of water in and out of the tank keeps fresh cool water before the rabbits at all times.

Install the pressure tank 1 foot or more above the highest hutch. If the supply pipe is raised to clear the feeding alleys, then install the tank about 1 foot above the highest point of the supply pipe.

courtesy USDA

A young rabbit using the automatic waterer.

47

Raised supply pipes may require vent pipes to keep the air bubbles out of the system. Install the vent pipe at the highest point in the supply line. See that the open end is at least 1 foot above the water in the tank. If it is necessary to change the level of the supply line from one row to another of hutches, use a piece of rubber hose to make the connection.

Determine the correct height for the tank by fastening a rubber hose to the tank outlet and then to the supply pipe. Raise or lower the tank until the valves, or dewdrops, from which the rabbits drink have the proper tension. If there is too much tension or pressure on the valves, the rabbits will not be able to trip them. Under too little tension, the valves will drip.

The proper height for the water valve is 9 inches from the hutch floor for medium and heavy breeds, and 7 inches for the smaller breeds. The valve may be hung on the outside and at the back of the hutch so no water drips on the rabbits or on the hutch floor. An opening in the back of the hutch will permit the rabbit to use the valve.

When hutches are back to back, use one pipe for supplying water to both hutches. Use a four-way outlet and short nipples for installing the valve. You can install one drinking valve for each hutch by drilling and tapping the supply pipe, and then screwing the valve into it.

If you are not equipped to make the plumbing installation, substitute a 3/4-inch rubber hose for the 1/2-inch supply pipe. Cut a hole in the hose and screw in the valve. Plastic pipe may be used in a similar manner. If a rubber hose or plastic pipe is used, it should be hung on the outside of the hutch to minimize the possibility of damage due to chewing or gnawing.

Check the automatic watering system periodically, especially when you put a rabbit in a hutch that has been unoccupied for several days. When valves are not used, even for a few days, minerals in the water may cause them to stick. Rabbits learn to use the system readily, even the young ones just out of the nest box.

NEST BOXES

No one type of nest box is best suited for all conditions, but all should provide seclusion for the doe at kindling and comfort and protection for the young. Nest boxes should be large enough to prevent crowding and small enough to keep the young together. All types should provide good drainage and proper ventilation.

Two general kinds have been used extensively, the box type and the nail-keg type. If a nail keg is used, nail a 1-by-6-inch board across the open end of the keg, so that it covers one-third to one-half of the opening. Drill several 1-inch holes in the closed end of the keg for ventilation, and some 1/4-inch holes in the bottom for drainage.

Since nail kegs have become difficult to obtain, apple and pear boxes are frequently used. These may be fitted with tops or left open. In either case, an opening should be cut in one end at the top, or a portion of one end removed, to provide easy access for the doe and young. As an alternative, one end may be fitted with removable boards or slats so that, as the young begin to leave the nest, panels may be removed to allow the young to reenter the nest box.

Prefabricated nest boxes are available from many suppliers, and may be used with excellent results. Their one disadvantage is that in extremely cold climates extra care must be used to insure the warmth of the young.

Loss of young rabbits kindled in the winter can be largely prevented if you furnish proper nesting accommodations. If a doe reacts normally to her newborn litter by pulling enough wool to make a warm nest and by feeding her young, and if the nest box is well insulated, the young can survive temperatures as low as $-15°$ to $-20°$ F.

You can make a good type of winter nest box by placing a standard size nest box inside a larger box. Pack straw into the space between the small box and the larger one on all sides except the entrance and top. A lid of ordinary box wood covered on the under side with several layers of paper will supply the necessary top insulation. Make two or three holes, 1/2-inch to 3/4-inch in diameter, in the lid at the end opposite the opening to the nest box for ventilation and to prevent condensation within the nest box.

On the bottom of the inner box put one or two layers of corrugated cardboard or several thicknesses of paper to keep the newborn litter from coming in contact with the cold boards. Fill the nest box so completely with new, clean straw that the doe will have to burrow into it to form a cavity for the nest. Inspect the box daily for the first three or four days. If the cardboard or paper becomes damp from accumulated moisture, remove it promptly. Replace it if cold weather continues.

A simpler nest box for use in winter is a single box lined completely with one or two layers of corrugated cardboard and filled with straw.

COOLING BASKETS

During the heat of summer, the young rabbits may become too hot in their nest box and should be so situated that they may cool off. This is done most effectively with a cooling basket. During the day, the young are placed in this basket, or box, which is then hung inside the cage. At evening, the young are returned to the nest box so that the mother can take care of them.

four
Feeds

Healthy, productive rabbits require clean, wholesome food and a regular feeding schedule. When you have obtained your rabbits and have provided suitable housing for them, your next decision must be the type of feed to use.

The feed that you provide your animals will be determined largely by the plans that you have for your rabbitry. The geographical location of the rabbitry will also be a determining factor in your final decision. This chapter will deal only with feeds, while the next chapter will discuss how to properly feed the rabbits.

What do you feed your rabbits? There are a number of choices, some better than others. Each rabbit herd and each breed of rabbit presents certain problems and challenges. There are, however, certain guidelines that may be followed for success.

Water

All rabbits need a steady supply of clean, fresh water. A doe and her litter of eight young will drink more than a gallon of water in an average twenty-four hour day. Of course, the water needs of each rabbit vary, and at times will change from day to day for a particular rabbit. Never attempt to guess what rabbits will need, but always keep a full supply of water before them.

Do not give your rabbits surface water, or water that has been standing in an open container. Although the water may have been fresh early in the day, by evening the chance of contamination is great. The few extra steps necessary to provide clean water throughout the day are more than offset by the vigorous condition of the rabbit that has had sufficient clean water.

During freezing temperatures, it's best to take the chill from the water. Also, do not leave water containers in the hutch when there is a possibility of freezing. The simplest method of watering in a cold climate is to offer your rabbits water in the morning and evening, then remove the container when they have had their fill.

In warmer climates, and especially in hot

weather, try to keep the water containers out of the sun. It's not unusual for water to reach 100° F. when subjected to direct sunlight. Provide for the comfort and health of your rabbits at all times.

In the chapter on hutch equipment, I mentioned that some rabbitries use heat tape on the waterers to prevent freezing. If you are planning a large rabbitry and will use self-waterers, you will have little problem with freezing water. If you plan to have a small rabbitry, you will find it best to follow the general instructions given in this chapter. Although some rabbitmen have been successful in handling their water problems in other ways, the most economical and practical methods for the beginner are presented here.

Hay

Hay supplies the necessary fiber for a well-balanced ration. A good, high-quality hay will also provide most of the protein needed in a healthy diet.

Legume hays, including clover, alfalfa, cowpea, vetch, and peanut, are very high in protein and are palatable. These are the best if available. Grasses, such as timothy, prairie grass, Johnson grass, Sudan grass, and carpet grass, are good, but they are less palatable and contain approximately half as much protein as the legume hays. When feeding grass hays, you must add protein to the ration for proper balance.

All grass hays should be a green color and be free of mold. The use of moldy, damp, or dirty grass is an invitation to disease.

Fine-stemmed, leafy, well-cured hay may be fed to rabbits without cutting. Coarse hay should be chopped into 3-inch or 4-inch lengths to help the rabbits' digestion and to eliminate waste.

Grass cuttings from a newly mowed lawn may be fed as part of the ration so long as the grass has not been sprayed with insecticide.

Grains

A number of small and large rabbitries successfully feed a variety of grains to their herd. Oats, barley, wheat, soybean grain, buckwheat, rye, and a soft variety of corn may be fed whole or in milled form as part of the daily ration. Do not feed castor beans, or poppy, goldenrod, and oleander seeds. These are extremely harmful to the rabbit's digestive system.

The majority of grains are similar in food value. They may be substituted for one another without altering the nutritive value of the feed. Do not switch from one grain to another frequently, however. Establish a schedule using certain grains and attempt to stay with it.

In using grains, it's wise to avoid feeding your rabbits finely ground feed. The small particles enter the rabbit's nostrils, causing sneezing and irritation.

Although some rabbitries continue to use grains and alfalfa as feed, the most progressive and successful rabbitmen have discontinued their use, primarily because of the time involved in feeding. Storing grain, grass, and hay through climatic changes, and protecting it from mold, rodents, and insects, are also time consuming.

Supplements

When you feed your rabbits hay and grain, it is necessary to add a supplement to the daily ration to provide proper nutrition. This may be in the form of soybean, peanut, or linseed meals, which are all rich in protein. It's important to determine a proper ration and to add whatever supplements are necessary if you want healthy rabbits.

Salt

Rabbits require a certain percentage of salt in their daily diet. Since this requirement may vary in different rabbit herds and in different geographical areas, it may be supplied by attaching small salt spools to the side of the hutch. A rabbit can lick the salt as desired. Do not position these salt spools so that they touch wire or metal cage parts. Contact of salt with metal will cause corrosion.

If salt spools are not available, the salt requirement may be supplied by adding 0.5 to 1 percent fine salt to the mixed feed as needed.

Table Scraps

When only a few rabbits are kept as pets, it's possible to feed them directly with scraps from your table. Be sure to determine whether these scraps provide a balanced meal. If not, the missing nutrients should be provided to insure healthy animals.

Uncooked leftovers, such as vegetable greens, carrot and beet tops, lettuce, and potato peelings, are beneficial to the rabbit. Various fruits such as apples and pears may be fed. The rabbit may also be given stale bread that does not contain mold.

Do not feed rabbits spoiled, sour, or greasy leftovers. Never feed them meat scraps, fresh or cooked. Although rabbits will eat meat scraps, they usually are not acceptable to the animal's digestive system, and sickness results. When you feed leftovers, remember that the rabbit is not a garbage disposal unit. Use common sense in feeding. The goal of a good rabbitry should always be healthy animals: fresh, wholesome food is the way to achieve this goal.

Commercial Feeds

More than three-fourths of the rabbit owners in the United States, from the person who has one pet rabbit to the owner of a large commercial rabbitry of five thousand or more animals, use commercial feeds exclusively. They have been proven to be easier, more economical, and in the long run to have more nutritional value per daily ration than hay and grain.

The brand and type of commercial feed to use is up to you. Check with other breeders and hobbiests in your area to find out what they have been most successful with in feeding. Also, when you purchase your rabbits, consider using the type feed the breeder you buy from uses. In fact, if you have no other rabbits in your rabbitry, you will be better off using the same feed. Otherwise you must provide a gradual change-over of feed, which may prove difficult to do successfully if you are a beginner.

If you live in an area where there is no opportunity to choose from a variety of feeds, don't be concerned. As long as the feed that is available is fresh and clean, it will be sufficient for raising healthy animals. Most commercial

feeds contain the necessary nutritional requirements for successful growth; the majority
exceed this requirement by a large margin.

When you purchase commercial feed,
follow the company's printed instructions that
accompany the feed. All feed companies also
publish helpful booklets describing their feed.
You will find that they contain excellent instructions for the beginner, not only on how to feed
the rabbit herd but also on general care of the
rabbitry. Send for the booklets and use them.
You'll find a list of some of these companies in
the Appendix at the end of this book.

There are three basic types of commercial
feed that you should investigate. Choose what
you feel best suits your particular rabbitry program. Do not rush, rather, make a careful
choice. One factor that will influence your
choice is where you live. Supplements, for example, are available in rural areas but usually
not in cities.

The first type of commercial feed is the all-
grain pellet, which must have a quantity of hay
served with it to round out the diet
requirements. This is an excellent feed. You
must remember, however, that there will be additional expense and labor with feeding the hay.

Probably the most widely used commercial
feed is the complete ration pellet, which is

usually dark green in color. This pellet contains all the necessary nutritional requirements, produces a healthy rabbit, and promotes excellent growth in the young. The addition of hay to the diet is not needed when using this pellet.

Neither of the above types of pellet includes medication. When using either type, it is advisable to add medication to the water to help prevent disease. This is covered in more detail in the chapter on rabbit diseases and their prevention.

Finally, some manufacturers produce a complete ration pellet which includes all food requirements plus medication. Since all rabbits are highly susceptible to respiratory problems and the dreaded coccidiosis, medication placed in the pellet goes a long way towards a successful program of preventive medicine.

I have found that a medicated feed is the most successful feed to use and that the added cost is negligible. Feeding a medicated pellet will add about 3 1/2 cents to the cost of raising a rabbit to full maturity. This is a cheap price to pay for a healthy animal.

Remember, a correct feeding program is another key to a successful, healthy animal, that will provide strong litters and good meat for the table. Don't try to cut corners. Your rabbits will suffer; so will your pocketbook.

When purchasing feed, whether in 10, 25, 50, or 100 pound containers, do not accept a sack that has been opened and then taped or stapled shut. You are purchasing trouble. Let me illustrate. I purchased a 50 pound bag of feed that had been broken open and then resealed with masking tape and fed a number of rabbits from it that evening. The next morning five pedigreed Californians were dead of the bloat, all due to being fed rotten feed.

If you have any doubts about the feed, don't buy it. A fair and honest feed dealer will assist you in raising your rabbits successfully by selling only fresh feed. Do not purchase feed offered on sale or at special discounts. Cheap feed is no bargain.

A final word of instruction when using commercial feeds. When you open a new sack, remove the label from the bag and keep it until the feed has been used. If for some reason you suspect that the feed has caused sickness or death, the tag should immediately be sent to the feed company. They will be able to tell from the code stamped on the tag where and when it was produced.

Feed companies don't want problems with their feed. They are in business to make a profit and can't do so unless the feed they produce is satisfactory. They realize that one unhappy feed customer can ruin the effect of thousands of dollars worth of advertising.

Storage Space

All feed, whether hay, grain, or commercial feed, must be stored in an area that is rodent and insect proof. The feed must be kept dry and protected from contact with dogs, cats, rats, and chickens, carriers of disease to your rabbitry. When you open a sack of feed, have a container with a tight lid available to hold the contents. A plastic or galvanized garbage can, with a tight lid, provides effective and economical security for the feed.

Now that you have decided on the type of feed for your rabbit herd, your next question will probably be: "How do I feed them correctly?" This will be discussed in the next chapter.

five
Feeding

One of the most demanding and time-consuming jobs in running a rabbitry is the daily feeding of the herd. No matter how excellent and complete the feed may be, it is worthless unless fed correctly, on a proper schedule.

A regular schedule of feeding is much more important than whether the rabbits are fed one, two, or three times a day. A rabbit becomes accustomed to a set schedule and will show discomfort and restlessness when this schedule is not kept or is varied from day to day.

Remember, rabbits, both wild and domestic, are rodents that eat mostly at night. Therefore, many professional rabbitmen prefer a once-a-day feeding, either in late afternoon or early evening. They feel also that the rabbit benefits most when it can eat without being disturbed.

When you design a feeding schedule, whether for one or a hundred rabbits, decide on the best time for you to take care of your rabbitry. If you put off feeding when the weather is bad, or if you are away at feeding time, you are doing an injustice to the rabbits. If you don't have the time to take proper care of your rabbits, get rid of them and get a hobby that doesn't eat.

When a litter of young are with a doe, a schedule of morning and evening feedings is best. This provides a maximum amount of food for the family and encourages fast growth. If, when feeding on a twice-a-day schedule, you find some feed is not eaten, reduce the ration. Since rabbits are moody, much like humans, and are influenced by weather changes, their food intake will fluctuate.

The feeding requirements of your rabbits will vary. Dry does, herd bucks, and fryers will require a different quantity of feed than a doe with litter. Also, as mentioned earlier, climatic conditions will influence their food needs. A feeding program is successful when the herd is provided with food that is nutritious enough to keep it in top production and excellent health.

Different feeding requirements are shown

by the following statistics, taken from the United States Department of Agriculture Farmers Bulletin No. 1730, "Rabbit Production."

Feeding requirements for dry does, herd bucks, and developing young are:

	Percent of Ration
Protein	12 to 15
Fat	2 to 3.5
Fiber	20 to 27
Nitrogen-free extract	43 to 47
Ash or mineral	5 to 6.5

Rations for pregnant does and does with litters should contain more protein:

	Percent of Ration
Protein	16 to 20
Fat	3 to 5.5
Fiber	15 to 20
Nitrogen-free extract	44 to 50
Ash or mineral	4.5 to 6.5

Changes of Feed

Unless it is absolutely necessary, do not change the type of feed you are providing your rabbits. If you are feeding commercial feeds, do not change from one brand to another. The changing of feed has been known to cause death. Most rabbits, especially the young ones, are very sensitive to sudden changes in their diet. This is especially true when changing from green to commercial feeds. The digestive tract must have time to adjust.

If a change does become necessary, the following procedure will probably be the best and most practical to follow. Start by giving a small amount of the new feed approximately half an hour after the herd has had a scheduled meal (if fed twice a day). Gradually increase the amount of new feed, but be careful to watch for signs of ill effects (check the droppings). If no sign of trouble appears within a week, use the new feed entirely in the morning and gradually eliminate the old feed at night. Within two weeks have the herd on the new feed.

Another method is to start the feed transfer by mixing a very small amount of the new feed in with the old at feeding time. Each day increase the amount of new feed while decreasing the amount of old feed. Within ten to fourteen days, the switchover can be completed, and the herd has not suffered from a sudden switch.

Pregnant Does and Litters

After you determine that a doe is pregnant, give her all the food she will eat, adding a good quality hay if available. Don't forget to provide an ample water supply at all times.

The day the doe kindles, cut her food ration by one-half. Beginning on the third day, gradually increase her feed ration each day for five days. After the first week, keep feed in front of her at all times. At this point, many rabbitries add a creep-ration to the diet. This is a commercial feed that is designed to help the young make the transition from doe's milk to regular feed. Also, it enables the doe to keep in top physical condition.

When the young rabbits are three to four weeks old, they will begin to leave the nest box and start to eat the regular ration. Keep a good supply of feed in front of them at all times.

Re-Ingesting Food

All rabbits re-ingest their food, which means they eat their food a second time. This is usually done in the early morning when they are not being observed. They re-ingest only certain soft matter that has passed through the digestive tract. This is taken directly from the anus, chewed, and then swallowed.

Many rabbit breeders are unaware of this practice. Some who have observed it believe that it means the rabbit is lacking something in its diet. Re-ingesting is normal, however, and may actually add to the value of the food because it passes through the digestive tract a second time.

Grazing Rabbits

Although the practice of grazing rabbits is no longer being used by intelligent and knowledgeable rabbitmen, it should be mentioned briefly. A large investment is necessary to build the fences and enclosures required to safely house rabbits. Some rabbitmen have even tried using an enclosed garage.

There are no advantages to grazing rabbits while the disadvantages are numerous. For one, there is a continual problem of fighting between the mature bucks. Also, there is no possibility of keeping any type of accurate records. Mating continues uncontrolled, and when the young are old enough to move, there is no easy way to determine parentage. There is also the problem of continual breeding, which will lower the quality of the herd.

The idea of grazing rabbits is used primarily by rabbit brokers as a gimmick to sell rabbits. These people know this system is a waste of time and money, but they have no desire to do anything but get money from naive newcomers to the rabbit-raising world.

six
Sanitation

Prevention of disease through good sanitation practices is important to a healthy and successful rabbitry. Any other approach in striving for healthy animals and good production will be very costly and will not succeed over a period of time.

Good sanitation takes time to plan and carry out. Many new rabbit breeders and fanciers attempt to enlarge their rabbitry too fast, without figuring in the time necessary to give good care to their animals. It is important to remember that if you do not have enough time to keep your rabbitry clean, the only result will be odors, diseased animals, and a discouraged rabbit owner.

What is sanitation? Does it take any special

knowledge or training? The answers to both these questions are quite simple. Sanitation is keeping cages, waterers, and feeders clean, continually removing manure and replacing bedding, and watching for possible disease. The only requirement for a program of good sanitation is common sense. If you learn a few basic steps in disease control and put these ideas to work each day, correct sanitation will result. Let's take a look at what is involved in a program of rabbitry sanitation.

Good sanitation and disease control begin when you purchase your rabbits. If the animals you buy are not clean and disease free, you will only be moving the problems of the person who sold you the rabbits to your rabbitry. Although the subject of purchasing animals has been covered in another chapter, a few points should be mentioned again.

When you purchase animals, try to select a reliable breeder whose cages are clean and whose rabbits are free from disease. Select disease-resistant rabbits for pets or breeders, and they will pass to their young an ability to survive. Ask the breeder about his disease problems. A good breeder, particularly an American Rabbit Breeders Association member, will be more than glad to answer your questions honestly and frankly.

No matter how good the reputation of the breeder you buy from, always isolate your new rabbits for at least fourteen to twenty-one days in a separate hutch or cage placed at least 60 feet from your other rabbits. Also, after taking a rabbit to a show or placing it on display away from your rabbitry, isolate it for the same period. This will prevent the spread of any disease the rabbit may have picked up. It is possible for a healthy rabbit to be a carrier of disease.

In a successful sanitation program, regular cleaning of cages or hutches is probably the most important factor. This also will take the most time. Hutches should be cleaned and disinfected on a regular schedule. The type of hutch you are using, all-wood, wood and wire, or all-wire, will determine how much time you will need to spend.

The all-wood hutch is the most difficult to keep clean. With an all-wood floor, even those of slats, the bedding of hay, wood shavings, or other similar material must be kept clean, since the manure and urine is absorbed by the floor. If the bedding is not changed daily, the wood floor will become damp and will be a fertile field for many disease organisms.

The wood hutch with an all-wire floor is easier to maintain, since the manure and urine will naturally fall through it and into the catch pan or onto the ground. The wood sides, however, will still absorb some of the odor.

The all-wire cage is the easiest to keep

clean. All droppings fall through and there is no wood to absorb odors. Also, as mentioned previously, there is less of a maintenance problem.

Before you clean a hutch, the rabbit must be removed. Then use a stiff bristled brush, a scraper (putty knife), soap or detergent, and plenty of hot water to get into every corner where hair and manure are apt to collect. After scrubbing, rinse with cold water until all signs of the soap have disappeared. If you are not sure all the soap is washed away, rinse again. DO NOT RISK THE HEALTH OF YOUR RABBIT.

After you remove a rabbit or a litter from an all-wire cage, or a hutch with an all-wire floor, the best method of eliminating all chance of disease is to sear the wire with a small blow-torch. This destroys most organisms and guarantees the next occupant a clean home.

To disinfect the hutch, obtain a suitable disinfectant (lye or a strong liquid disinfectant) and dilute it properly for use. Apply it by spraying, brushing, or wiping with a rag (wear rubber gloves); in the case of waterers and feeders, the disinfectant may be poured into a large pan and the items immersed. Do not reuse any disinfectant. Once it has been applied, throw it away. There is no sense in trying to practice good sanitation while at the same time reusing a dirty solution of disinfectant. Most important to remember is to get a good disinfectant and then follow the instructions on the container.

Be sure to rinse all equipment with clean, cold water 30 to 60 minutes after the disinfectant has been applied. Do not use any solution on a hutch when rabbits are in it. No matter how safe the label claims the solution to be, do not risk the health of your animals.

Remember: To be effective, this cleaning and disinfecting must be done on a regular schedule at least once a week. Even if the cages look clean, go over them again. There are hundreds of germs there, invisible to the eye but very deadly.

All open waterers and feeders should be cleaned every day. Whether you use crocks, pans, or coffee cans, the health of a rabbit is determined by how clean these eating and drinking containers are.

The easiest method of cleaning these containers is to use soap and hot water. Thoroughly wash the containers and let them sit in the soapy solution for about 10 minutes. Then remove them and rinse in clear water. They can also be dipped in the same type of disinfectant used for the hutches.

Self-watering nipples and closed feeders should be cleaned once a week. The nipples on the self-waterers may be washed with soap and water and then disinfected without removing them from the connecting pipes. The self-feeders should be removed before cleaning.

It is important to remember that all types of waterers and feeders must be cleaned immediately if any foreign matter appears. This is especially true for the open waterers and feeders since many rabbits manage to get droppings in them. Also, if the feed becomes soft and wet, remove it. Most rabbits will not eat food in this condition.

Another piece of equipment that must be kept spotlessly clean is the nest box. More newborn young are lost because of dirty nest boxes than from any other cause.

Every nest box should be cleaned at three separate stages. Before the doe kindles, the box should be completely cleaned with soap and water, and then disinfected. When the young open their eyes and leave the nest during the day, the box should be taken out, cleaned, and returned. Finally, after the young no longer need the nest box, it should be removed, cleaned, disinfected, and then stored for future use.

Each nest box must be cleaned before a new litter arrives. Newborn rabbits are highly susceptible to disease and an infected nest box will be a source of trouble. While the nest box is in storage, there is always the possibility of a rat leaving droppings in it. A dirty nest box is a poor home for a new litter.

The removal of manure and soiled bedding should be carefully planned, then carried out on a regular schedule. The rabbitry that has only a handful of rabbits presents few problems in this area. The soiled bedding can be burned and used for fertilizer, or placed in a plastic disposal bag and left for the garbage collector. If the manure is not used for the garden or lawn, it may be flushed down the toilet with no danger of stopping up the sewer lines. The owner of a larger rabbitry must take more care in manure disposal.

When you are disposing of droppings, an important fact to remember is that rabbit manure is an excellent fertilizer. It may be placed directly on the garden or lawn without fear of burning the plants or grass. I have used it on various vegetables in my garden and the results have been very satisfying.

A regular schedule of manure and bedding removal will eliminate a problem that everyone should be concerned about—angry neighbors. The majority of neighbors are understanding and tolerant, but there are always a few that seem to go out of their way to be obnoxious. It is this type of neighbor that every rabbit lover must be on guard against.

When a neighbor calls a government agency and complains about the odor of your rabbitry, no end of problems may result. Even when you have complied with all local zoning ordinances, your rabbitry may be declared a nuisance. Once investigated, you are on the books as a messy operator and no matter what happens in the neighborhood from then on the blame seems always to be placed on your rabbitry.

How do you eliminate this problem? Good sanitation. The following hints will prove helpful. (1) Do not remove manure on a windy day. The odor travels. (2) If the odor begins to become noticeable and you cannot remove the manure immediately, use an odor-masking spray over the entire area. This spray is also helpful in hot weather. (3) Always provide good ventilation.

To help remove odors and at the same time to increase the value of their rabbitries, a number of rabbitmen have developed worm beds under their hutches. Usually the worm beds work fine, especially in the warmer climates, but they do at times become a harbor for rats and flies. In colder climates during the winter months, the worms crawl deep in the beds, allowing the fresh manure to build up on top. The manure on top is in a raw state, and when the first warm spell occurs, the odor becomes almost unbearable.

Moving diseased animals away from healthy ones and immediately disposing of dead rabbits are also important to successful sanitation. Any rabbit that is sick or suspected of having an infection or a disease should be separated from the rest of the herd. As mentioned before, a place approximately 60 feet away from the main herd is recommended.

Any rabbit that dies from a known infection should be disposed of quickly. All equipment should be disinfected and the rabbit, its bedding, plus its droppings should be burned.

If an animal dies of an unknown disease, and there is a veterinarian or an animal laboratory in the area, pack the animal in ice to prevent deterioration and get an autopsy performed to learn the cause of death.

Don't loan rabbits. I have been asked many times to loan bucks for mating and have always refused to do so. Also, do not agree to allow a strange doe to be mated in your buck's cage unless the owner agrees that you may first isolate that doe for the regular isolation period of fourteen to twenty-one days. Be cautious of outside people, especially other rabbit raisers, visiting your rabbitry. People can be disease carriers.

Remember, preventing a disease through using proper sanitation measures is far cheaper and easier than treating a sick rabbit. Good sanitation? It's really not hard.

seven
Breeding

A successful rabbitman, whether he raises one or a hundred rabbits, must create and follow a practical breeding plan. Without correct breeding practices, such factors as sanitation, housing, and feeding will mean absolutely nothing.

The subject of breeding would fill many volumes, but if you follow the basic rules of breeding as outlined in this chapter, your chances for success are excellent. If you are more advanced in your knowledge of rabbit raising, and have an interest in such areas as genetics, germ cells, and heredity, you should obtain more advanced texts.

First Mating

The breed of your rabbit and its physical development will determine the correct age to begin mating. Although animal husbandry experts have determined the best minimum age to begin mating the various breeds, each rabbit usually gives an indication when it is ready. It is always wiser to go by the development of an individual rabbit for the first mating than to follow a rigid schedule.

Generally, the smaller breeds are sexually ready between five and six months of age, with the Polish an early starter at four months. The medium-weight rabbits, such as the New Zealand and the Californian, are usually ready at six to eight months. The heavy breeds, such as the Flemish Giant, are not mature until the age of eight to ten months.

Although many young bucks will attempt to mate at an early age, it is best to try to prevent this from occurring. In many cases when an underage buck serves a doe successfully, the young are small in size, abnormalities show up, or there are few babies to the litter. This is one reason why most breeders separate young bucks as soon as possible from does.

Just as it is important to prevent a rabbit from mating at too early an age, it is also important that you not wait too long to mate for the first time. A past due doe is usually hard to mate and often must be force-mated. The young do not seem to be as healthy as the young of other does, and a number of problems crop up that do not appear when the doe is mated at the correct time in her development.

Breeding Schedule

The breeding schedule you follow will be determined largely by your plans for the rabbitry. If you plan to raise rabbits primarily for show, two litters per doe a year is recommended. Try to arrange the matings so that the young will be of the proper age to enter the various classes of competition.

Those who are interested in raising meat animals can step up the matings considerably. Rabbits have a gestation period of approximately one month. This plus the two month weaning period gives the possibility of four litters a year if no passes occur.

Some breeders are successful with as many as six litters per year, but the beginner is advised not to attempt such a schedule. If you set up a breeding schedule of six litters per doe, it will be necessary to breed the doe approximately two weeks after kindling. When a doe is bred this soon, the litter must be removed no later than five weeks after birth so that the doe can build her nest again.

Little physical harm is likely to occur with frequent breeding. Some breeders insist that the doe wears out somewhat earlier, while others claim that the doe stays healthier. As with other issues of rabbit raising, there are two opposing views.

The most important fact to consider when breeding any rabbit is its health. If both doe and buck are free of disease, are not skinny or over-weight, and have good vitality, breeding will come naturally in the majority of cases. Don't ever sacrifice the health of any rabbit to secure a litter of young.

Occasionally, a litter is lost shortly after kindling. The practice at the Double D Rabbitry has been to rebreed the doe immediately on the fifth day following the loss. Many experts in the field of animal husbandry declare that by rebreeding immediately, the breeder is doing the doe a favor.

Mating

When you are ready to mate a rabbit, take time to determine whether it is in good health. The majority of does give outward signs of being ready to mate, such as restlessness, rubbing their chin on the hutch or water crock, and attempting to reach nearby rabbits. While these signs may be used by the fancier or small rabbitry owner, it is not practical for the large-scale breeder.

If you set up a regular schedule, more litters will be kindled, and the guesswork will be eliminated. Records are very important at this stage; there should be a separate card filled out for each doe and buck in the rabbitry. (Refer to the chapter entitled "Keeping Records" and follow the instructions given there for best results.)

Many successful rabbitries use a buck for mating only once every three or four days. My own experiments have shown that when a buck is used more than twice in a single day, there are more passes or misses, and the litters that do kindle are smaller in number of young. For this reason, one buck should be provided for every ten does for maximum results.

Always take the doe to the buck's cage for service. The majority of does will not allow a strange rabbit in their cage, and may attack and severely injure the buck. When you place the doe with the buck, mating will probably occur immediately. If not, leave the doe and buck together for 5 minutes or so before deciding whether to force-mate the doe or to return her to her cage.

Even if a buck attempted to service a doe but did not show signs of actually having done so, it is wise to make a notation of the attempt. I have been surprised a few times when a litter suddenly showed up and no indication of a possible mating had been entered on the hutch card. Apparently, sperm had been ejected close enough to the vulva to impregnate the doe. As many rabbitmen will attest, rabbits can be full of surprises.

When mating does occur, the buck will fall on his side. Usually he will also show a physical reaction such as squealing, stamping, or jerking his body; do not use these reactions as definite signs that actual impregnation has resulted, however.

Some rabbitries have the practice of breeding the doe twice in the same day. If this program is followed, the doe should be returned to the buck's cage approximately five hours after the first service. I have also visited rabbitries where the practice is to leave the doe with the buck all day. This can be dangerous since two mature rabbits will fight.

Neither of these practices are recommended for the beginner. Follow the practices used by the most knowledgeable and successful rabbitmen for best results. As you learn more about your rabbits and their habits, you may experiment with other ideas.

Forced Matings

There will always be some does who will refuse to accept normal service from a buck. At times even the does who are usually cooperative will have nothing to do with any buck; they will sit in a corner on their tail. These does must be restrained for mating.

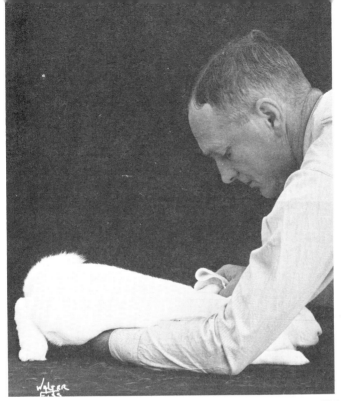

A doe may be restrained for mating when service is not promptly accepted. Notice the position of the hands when holding the doe and when supporting and elevating the hindquarters.

To restrain a doe, use your right hand to hold the ears and a fold of skin over the shoulders. Place your left hand under the body and between the hind legs. Then place your thumb on the right side of the vulva, index finger on the left side, and push the skin gently backward. This procedure throws the tail up over the back, exposing the opening. Support the weight of the rabbit with your left hand and elevate the hindquarters to the normal height for service by the buck.

Bucks and does who are accustomed to being handled will not object to this assistance. The buck may, however, sniff your hand and turn away without mounting the doe; the problem may be solved by rubbing both hands on the rabbit's fur, thus disguising the human odor.

It is always best to hold the doe the first few times a young buck is used. This will speed matings and insure service in the more difficult cases. Do not expect complete success in every case with the restrained doe. But, by using this system, you will notice a definite increase in the number of successful matings.

Gestation

The period of time from mating to kindling, called the gestation period, is usually thirty-one or thirty-two days. Some litters may be born as early as the twenty-eighth day, and some as late as the thirty-fifth day. In the average rabbitry, between 98 and 99 percent of all litters are born on the thirty-first day.

When kindling is delayed past the thirty-second day, the litter is apt to contain a few young that are larger than usual or have various abnormalities, or some of the young may be born dead.

The most practical way to solve the problem of does who kindle late litters with abnormalities is to eliminate these does from the herd. Of course, the does should be given a second chance to produce quality litters, since one abnormal litter could be the result of a temporary problem. I have found definite indications that this trait is passed from generation to generation and should, therefore, be closely watched.

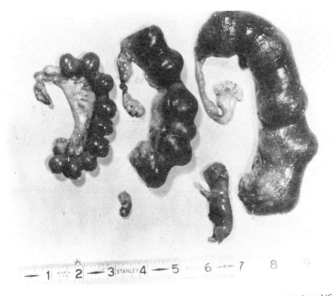

courtesy USDA

Uteri from three does showing embryonic development of ten, fourteen, and twenty-one day pregnancies. The ten-day embryo is so small that it is difficult to see.

89

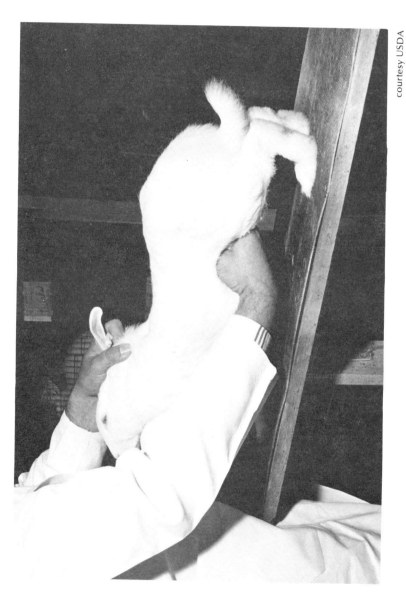

courtesy USDA

The correct and most successful method of determining pregnancy.

Determining Pregnancy

A number of methods are being advocated to determine whether a doe has conceived. There is only one way, however, that has proven to be reliable in the majority of cases. But first, let's examine two questionable practices.

Probably the most unreliable test is to examine the doe for a gain in overall flesh and for swelling of the abdominal region. Only toward the end of the gestation period can this procedure be fairly indicative, and if the doe does not prove to be pregnant, valuable time has been lost in the breeding schedule.

The second method, which is somewhat more reliable, is test mating. Here the doe is returned to the buck's cage about the eighteenth day after mating. If the doe avoids the buck, or fights and whines, she may be pregnant. However, although pregnant she may accept the buck again, or, even though she is not pregnant, she may refuse to allow the buck to serve her. This system as you can see is unpredictable and should not be relied on in a progressive rabbitry.

The most successful way to determine pregnancy is to examine the doe twelve to fourteen days after mating. Gently restrain the doe with one hand and with the other cupped forward feel the doe's abdomen. If the doe is pregnant, the young will feel like small marbles. Avoid using too much pressure for at this stage the unborn are easily damaged. If no young are present inside the doe, return her to the buck for further service.

False Pregnancy

Occasionally a doe is mated, and sheds her egg cells, but does not become pregnant. This may be caused by the buck being sterile at the time of mating, the doe being in a cage next to a buck, or the doe being ridden by another doe in the same cage. There is nothing that can be done when false pregnancy occurs. You must wait out the usual seventeen-day false pregnancy period and then attempt to mate the doe again. While experiencing this period of false pregnancy, the doe will avoid the buck and if he does manage to service her, she will be unable to conceive.

At the end of the seventeen-day period, the doe will pull hair and attempt to build a nest. By the twentieth to twenty-second day, she will show signs of being ready to mate.

Barren Periods

Unlike their wild cousins, most domestic rabbits will breed throughout the year. The natural breeding season is spring and early summer, but by successful cross breeding and genetic development man has been able to practically eliminate the barren periods. But, from time to time and for one reason or another, a doe or buck is unable to mate. There are several reasons for this.

The female rabbit has a heat cycle that lasts about sixteen days. During this cycle, breeding usually results in pregnancy. The two days before and two days after this period are times when changes are taking place in the eggs. Breeding at these times may not result in pregnancy.

Periods up to four to ten weeks may occur when a buck will lose interest in mating or a doe will not conceive. A doe may go as long as four months without kindling any young. These cases, however, are mostly due to the rabbit's poor physical condition, usually a result of poor nutrition.

Another possible cause for a barren condition is extreme temperature, especially a sudden change to a higher one. Some rabbits react to these changes by becoming barren for a period of time.

Inbreeding

Inbreeding is the practice of mating animals that are closely related, such as father and daughter, or brother and sister. In the hands of a knowledgeable rabbit breeder, it is a very effective way to strengthen the breeding stock. The average fancier or a beginner, however, does not have the experience to judge the best qualities in his stock, plus he does not have the formal training in genetics necessary for successful results.

If the rabbitman has extra stock available for experimentation, there is no reason why inbreeding could not be tried. Although the first results usually will be discouraging, the experience gained might benefit the entire rabbitry.

When following a program of inbreeding, you should determine at the beginning that there are no outstanding weaknesses in those rabbits being bred. Although inbreeding is used to intensify the best points of a rabbit, keep in mind that the practice also intensifies the poor qualities in the animal's heredity.

Line Breeding

Line breeding has proved to be the most satisfactory method of improving the herd and has the highest ratio of results. The process is similar to inbreeding except that the matings are between rabbits not so closely related. The line breeding method eliminates many of the unknown factors prevalent in other breeding methods, and is the one recommended for a beginner.

Line breeding makes it possible to develop

desired characteristics in a herd. A record of long life, heavy milk production, and disease resistance in the rabbit being bred will be passed on and further developed in the offspring. Remember that the opposite, however, is also true. Weaknesses such as low milk production or low resistance to disease may show up in the offspring and will at times show up in future generations. By constant selective breeding and culling of any young that are not exactly what's wanted, you can increase the possibility of removing unwanted traits more effectively than with other breeding practices.

Cross Breeding

Cross breeding is the practice of breeding purebred rabbits of different breeds to obtain a specialized result. The offspring are not usually good stock, and even members of the same litter vary as to characteristics.

Considerable experimentation has been done in the field of cross breeding, with both failure and success as results. An example of success in this method is the Californian, which has become an excellent show and meat animal.

There is always room for improvement in the various breeds, and what has been written here is not meant to discourage those really interested. The newcomer, however, should spend his time studying what has been done in the past and learning all there is to know about the animals in his herd. Then he is ready to experiment.

Artificial Insemination

Artificial insemination in commercial rabbitries is not presently being conducted on a large scale. The reasons probably are: few rabbitmen understand the process; a special knowledge of the reproductive organs is necessary; and considerably more time is required than for standard mating procedures. The possibilities of this practice, however, should not be overlooked by the serious rabbit raiser.

Artificial insemination would be of great value to the breeder who has an outstanding buck with a record of top-rated offspring. Since the reproductive life of many bucks is not much over two years, artificial insemination would enable more does to be served during the buck's period of highest potency, making greater herd development possible.

This book is geared primarily to newcomers to the field of rabbit raising, so a discussion of the subject in more detail would be of no real value. Those interested in knowing more about artificial insemination should refer to "Commercial Rabbit Raising," Bulletin 309, United States Department of Agriculture.

eight
Kindling

Very few complications occur with kindling as long as the rabbit is in good physical condition, has adequate housing, and is free of disease.

Just before it is time to kindle, the doe may eat very little. Be sure that there is plenty of fresh water for her. After she kindles, she should be fed sufficient food to supply the necessary nourishment for herself and her young.

Most litters are kindled at night. As each baby is born, the doe will lick it clean and nurse it. Immediately after kindling, the doe will usually be restless. Do not disturb her until she has quieted down, which may take as long as two days.

Do not imagine that because you don't see the doe nursing her young she is neglecting

A litter of newborn rabbits. Notice the hair that lines the nest.

them. A doe usually goes into the nest box early in the morning and late in the evening to nurse for a few minutes.

The Nest Box

Place the nest box in the hutch about twenty-seven days after mating. Fill the nest box two-thirds full with a nesting material such as clean straw, wood shavings, dry leaves, or loose grass. The doe will then make her nest, and by the time she kindles she will be accustomed to the box and will give birth in it satisfactorily.

Immediately before the doe kindles, she will remove fur from her breast and line the nest with it. After the young are born, she usually covers them with a layer of this fur. A doe may become lazy, however, and pull little or no fur. It is a good practice to store excess fur for times like this, and add it to the nest box when needed. When a doe pulls excessive amounts of hair, remove some and place it in a burlap sack. This sack could be secured to a hook on the wall, ready for the next lazy doe. The majority of does do not seem to mind strange fur being placed in their cage.

When the litter is approximately two weeks old, remove half of the nest material so that the nest will not be so crowded and at the same time the litter will have some protection. In four to five weeks, the nest box may be removed, completely cleaned, and stored for future use.

Care of the Young

On the second day following kindling, gently remove the hair and straw covering the newborn and check to determine whether any are dead or deformed. These should be removed and disposed of. Also determine the number of young in the litter and record this on the hutch card.

Many rabbitmen remove the underdeveloped young from the litter and dispose of them too. Their claim is that such a rabbit is unprofitable. At the Double D Rabbitry, we do not agree with this action. We feel that if a rabbit is not deformed but is only undersized it should be given a chance to survive. After allowing it to stay with the doe for about six weeks, we remove it and for a week or two feed it separately. Normally the rabbit will develop to its full size. Although this rabbit would be unsuitable as a breeder, it could be sold as a pet or a fryer. The added cost of taking care of such an animal is figured in the overall cost of running the rabbitry. This is, of course, our practice and we realize that each rabbitman will follow his own convictions.

If for any reason the litter is divided, the two nests must be made into one. A doe will nurse only one group of young and will completely ignore any of her young that might be in another nest in the same nest box. Unlike a cat who moves her young from place to place, a doe will not pick up her young and carry them to the nest.

From time to time a newborn rabbit will be found apparently lifeless outside the nest box. At the Double D Rabbitry, we have constructed a simple small wooden box with a bulb in the center of the lid. The lifeless rabbit is placed in the box on a bed of hay and the light turned on. The bulb should be about 6 to 8 inches above the animal so that enough heat is generated to warm it. Many times a rabbit has been saved by this action. When you return the young to the nest, rub your hands on the mother's fur, lightly rub the baby in the loose hair in the nest box, and then quietly add it to the litter. Very few times will the mother reject the baby.

Young rabbits generally will open their eyes ten to eleven days after birth. Occasionally, however, their eyes become infected and fail to open normally. If this infection is treated immediately, the rabbit will usually recover without eye injury.

Use warm water to bathe the infected eye. As the tissue around the eye softens, begin to separate the eyelids with slight pressure from the fingers. If pus shows around the eye after the lids are open, use an antibiotic eye ointment to treat the eye. With proper inspection and care from kindling to weaning, the litter and the doe should be healthy, have the proper weight, and have a good coat.

Caked Breast

Caked breast must be treated immediately to insure the good health of the doe. This condition may occur if the doe's milk is not being taken from the breast in sufficient quantities, or if the doe is injured and refuses to allow the young to nurse. Also, if a litter is weaned abruptly after only one month, the doe may develop slightly swollen and caked udders.

The first symptom of caked breast is "pink breast." The normal skin color turns pink, then red. At the same time, the breast becomes feverish and very firm and hard. As caked breast grows worse, the tissues around the teats enlarge. The skin darkens, the ends of the teats become tender and discolored, and the doe refuses to nurse.

To remedy caked breast, rub lanolin on each infected teat and massage the breast. You may also remove some of the milk from the teat, but be careful not to use too much pressure.

Litter Deaths

In every rabbitry, whether backyard or commercial, a certain number of young will be born dead or will die shortly after birth. Good herd management will help eliminate the great majority of these deaths. The percentage of young born dead or deformed can be lessened by proper care of the doe during gestation. Good housing, a quiet atmosphere, and careful handling all help the doe have healthy young.

Those young that die after birth usually do so because of one of the following three causes:

1. The doe was disturbed by predators (cats, dogs, snakes, opossums). This may cause her to kindle prematurely.

2. The doe was disturbed after kindling. The normal reaction of a rabbit that is disturbed is to stamp its feet hard on the floor of the cage. If the doe does this, she could injure or kill the young in the nest box.

3. The doe fails to produce milk or produces it in too small a quantity. Without milk, the young will starve within two days. They must immediately be fostered to a nursing doe.

Cannibalism

From time to time, a doe will eat her young, which can be caused by a number of factors: the doe has been given an inadequate ration, either in quality or in quantity; the doe is disturbed after kindling; the doe is from a strain that shows very little natural maternal instinct. If you handle the doe properly during her pregnancy and keep her quiet before and after kindling, this problem is not likely to develop.

Before condemning the doe for cannibalism, determine if dogs or cats are able to get close enough to the cages to kidnap the young. If you keep the cages well off the ground and enclose the entire rabbit compound with fencing, the problem of dogs can be eliminated. Certain types of fencing will also keep out cats.

Rats are a problem in cities and suburbs, and in rural areas. These rodents are fast and are intelligent enough to determine how to kidnap the young rabbits. They also carry many diseases. Although much of the rat problem can be eliminated by using properly designed and well-built cages, other means should be used to rid the area of these pests. Such devices as traps, powder, and poisoned food should be used.

In rural areas there are other pests such as opossums and snakes. Constant supervision and inspection, together with well-made hutches, help make the newborn young safe.

Even if the doe is known to have eaten some of her young, give her a second chance. If she practices cannibalism a second time, she should be destroyed.

Orphaned Litters and Fostering the Young

When a doe kindles more young than she can nurse at one time, the excess young should be fostered to other nursing does. This fostering of young can be done safely up to the age of one week. The safest time is twenty-four to thirty-six hours after kindling. Fostering of newborn young is made simpler when two or more does are mated on the same day. This usually provides at least one nursing doe for the excess newborn.

Sometime during a rabbitman's experience, a doe will die at kindling or before her young are able to eat by themselves. Some fanciers and commercial rabbitmen do not make an effort to keep these young alive. I believe, however, that an attempt should be made to raise the orphans. The decision will be yours to make.

Since a young rabbit does not open its eyes for ten days, an orphan cannot find a nipple on its own but must be fed by hand. An eyedropper or a doll's bottle can be used to feed it. Use either cow's or goat's milk for best results. A milk substitute such as the one sold for feeding young calves may be fed to the young rabbits if milk is not available.

Heat the milk until it is warm to the touch. Hold the baby gently and allow it to suck on the eyedropper or bottle. Do not overfeed. Too much milk will kill it. Remember, the nursing doe stays with her young only a few minutes at a time, so just a few drops of milk should be given the orphan at each feeding.

As the young begin to open their eyes, they will learn to drink from a small dish and, at the same time, will be attracted to the regular feed kept in the hutch.

Determining Sex

Sexing, or determining sex, may be done successfully by an experienced rabbitman when a rabbit is only a few days old. The beginner, however, is advised to wait until the young are ready for weaning, when the sex organs are more pronounced and are more easily determined. As you become more experienced, you should practice sexing a few young in the four-week-old stage of development. Gradually, by handling younger rabbits each time, you will develop enough skill to distinguish the sex of rabbits as young as two days old.

In the small rabbitry, early determination of sex is not necessary since most of the young will be kept either for pets or breeders or will be sold for fryers.

To determine sex, use your thumb and forefinger to gently press down around the sex organs. This will expose the inner surface of the opening. In the doe, a round opening appears with a slight depression near the anus. In the buck, the inner surface forms a circle.

Castration

The castration of a rabbit is quite simple for the professional rabbitman, but I do not advise the beginner to attempt it. In fact, unless you are raising Angora rabbits and are keeping a number of bucks for their wool, there is no real advantage in castrating the animals.

If, however, a rabbitman does want to castrate his bucks, I advise him to obtain a good book on animal husbandry or to contact a reliable breeder who can demonstrate the safest method. Castration is beyond the scope of this book.

Weaning the Litter

When a litter is three to four weeks old, the young will venture from the nest box and begin to eat regular food. This is to be encouraged, since the combination of the mother's milk and feed helps the young to develop to proper size and weight by weaning time.

courtesy USDA

Correct method of holding young fryers.

In many of the larger breeds, each litter will contain one or two that gain weight faster than the others. Remove these heavier animals as soon as they reach the desired weight, disregarding their age. This allows more milk for the remaining young.

By the time the young are eight weeks old, they should be taken from the doe and placed in a separate cage. It is a good idea to separate the does and the bucks at this time. The mother doe should be rebred at this time too.

Normally, the nursing doe will dry up as her young are weaned. Exceptional milkers may not, however. If this happens, leave one or two of the young with her as long as necessary.

All rabbits being raised for market should be ready by the end of eight weeks. After that time, the cost of feeding them increases, while the profit margin decreases. This does not, of course, include those young being kept for breeders.

nine
Diseases, Parasites, and Illnesses

Disease should not occur frequently in a well-managed rabbitry. In this chapter, various diseases and ailments will be discussed, and an attempt will be made to give in some detail the accepted methods of treatment. It must be remembered that I am not a veterinarian. The diagnoses and treatments presented here, however, are generally accepted and followed by most commercial rabbitries. A good rabbitman can readily tell when one of his animals is not well. This requires frequent inspection of the rabbit herd.

You may not find it easy at first to recognize symptoms and danger signs, but you will learn with experience. Examine your animals each day when feeding and watering them.

109

Note their food and water consumption and the color, consistency, and quantity of the droppings. Check the color and appearance of the hair coat, the brightness and general condition of the eyes, the way the rabbits move, their breathing, nasal discharge, and the condition of their ears.

Isolate sick animals immediately and keep them in isolation until they recover. Do not handle sick animals until after you have cared for the healthy ones. All dead animals should be buried or burned.

When a disease occurs in your rabbit herd, consult a veterinarian. He will be able to advise you on whether or not treatment will be practical, and if so, what the best procedure may be. He may also be able to make arrangements for additional diagnostic services at one of the animal disease laboratories operated by state departments of agriculture.

Be sure the veterinarian knows the value of the rabbit involved, so that he can recommend treatments that are practical under your conditions. Generally you can take a sick animal to the veterinarian's office. In some unusual cases, the veterinarian may want to visit your rabbitry. But remember, a house call will cost you more than an office visit.

Diseases are caused by living organisms, such as bacteria, protozoa, fungi, and viruses. Some of these organisms may be present in a seemingly healthy animal and will not cause illness unless something lowers the animal's resistance. Other organisms will make the animal sick immediately. A few of the conditions that can lower an animal's resistance are drafts, heat, cold, overfeeding, underfeeding, overhandling, sudden changes of location and feeding practices, crowding, and poor nutrition. These are sometimes called "predisposing causes" or "stress factors."

Many diseases have symptoms in common. An unskilled eye may not be able to determine whether an illness is serious or minor, and losses could be severe before the proper treatment is administered. Get advice from your veterinarian when there is doubt about the nature of the illness, when a death occurs suddenly, or when the illness persists. Consult with your veterinarian before your rabbits are sick. He may be able to advise you on disease control practices that are important in your part of the country.

You will remember that in Chapter 6, "Sanitation," considerable emphasis is placed on clean hutches and equipment. Cleanliness does prevent disease. Good sanitation will result in healthy, alert rabbits, whether they are being raised for show, meat, or breeding.

On the following pages, a number of diseases and injuries, symptoms, and possible treatments are described. By reading over this material carefully, you may be able to solve many health problems yourself. When in doubt, call a veterinarian.

Injuries

Injuries, often resulting in paralyzed hindquarters, usually result from improper handling or from the animal slipping in the hutch while exercising or while attempting to escape predators (especially around kindling time). Slipping usually happens at night. Common injuries are dislocated vertebrae, damaged nerve tissue, or strained muscles or tendons. If the injury is mild, the animal may recover in a few days. Make the rabbit comfortable and feed it a balanced diet. If it does not improve within a week, destroy it to prevent unnecessary suffering.

It is important that your rabbitry be quiet, comfortable, and protected from unnecessary disturbances that might cause the rabbits to be frightened.

Toenails

The toenails of rabbits that are confined in hutches do not wear down normally. They may even become long enough to cause foot deformity or to catch in the wire mesh floor. Periodically cut the nails with side-cutting pliers. Cut below the top of the cone in the toenail.

The cone can be observed by holding the foot up to a light. If the cone is cut, hemorrhaging or serious injury to the sensitive portion will occur.

Sore Dewlap

During warm weather, the dewlap, the fold of skin under the chin, may become sore. This happens when the rabbit drinks from a crock, constantly wetting the fur on the dewlap so that it gets muddy and foul-smelling. The skin on the dewlap and on the inside of the front legs becomes rough and the fur there may be shed. The animal usually scratches the irritated area, causing abrasions and infection.

Remove the cause by placing a board or a brick under the water crock to raise it so that the dewlap will not get wet when the rabbit drinks. If the skin becomes infected, clip off the fur and treat the area with a medicated ointment until the irritation clears up. The best solution to the problem is to use an automatic dewdrop watering system which eliminates the possibility of wet dewlap.

Colds or Sniffles (Rhinitis)

Colds and sniffles may be caused by a number of things. Drafts, heat, cold, poor ventilation, bacteria, viruses, allergies, and dietary deficiencies have all been found to bring on colds and sniffles in rabbit herds.

Sneezing and a runny nose are the main

113

courtesy Dr. Karl W. Hagen

Colds or sniffles will produce this result.

symptoms. The nasal discharge may be watery to very thick. The animal will frequently wipe its nose with its front paws, causing the fur on the paws to be wet or matted. There may be a discharge from the rabbit's eyes and its temperature is often below normal. Animals suffering from sniffles very often develop pneumonia.

To effectively control and treat the

problem, remove the infected animal from the rabbitry and isolate it. Commercial nose drops that are used for other animals or for human beings, containing either sulfuthzol, tetracycline, or oxtetracycline, are beneficial. Put two or three drops in each nostril morning and night.

Pneumonia

Pneumonia is an inflammation of the lungs that accompanies many diseases. Sometimes it occurs as a primary disease. It may be caused by chilling, infection, parasites, poison, or inhalation of gases and liquids.

The symptoms of pneumonia are obvious. The animal doesn't eat and has difficulty breathing, body temperature generally is elevated, and the head may be extended to relieve breathing. Death may occur soon after the illness begins.

To treat pneumonia, it is necessary to have an accurate diagnosis, so consult a veterinarian. A number of drugs are used, depending upon the cause. Sulfa drugs and antibiotics are useful in hastening recovery.

Enteritis or Scours

Scours, or diarrhea, generally is a symptom of some infection of the intestines (enteritis) caused by parasites, bacteria, viruses, incorrect feeding, poor digestion, or poisons.

115

Droppings range in consistency from semisolid to liquid, and blood may or may not be present. Generally a foul odor is present. The hair around the tail and back legs becomes soiled or matted. If the diarrhea is not checked in a short time, the animal will lose its body fluids and salts and become emaciated, and the hair coat will have a ruffled, dull appearance.

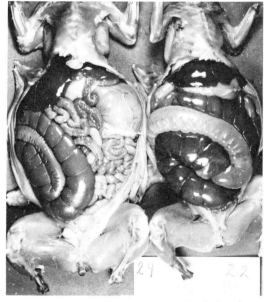

courtesy Dr. Karl W. Hagen

On the left is the normal condition of a rabbit's entrails at age forty-four days; the rabbit weighed 2.9 pounds. At the right is a rabbit of the same age with mucoid enteritis. That rabbit weighed only 2.2 pounds.

116

The correct treatment for enteritis depends on its cause. If it is due to parasites, the parasites should be removed with the proper drugs. A laxative such as castor oil may be used in case the enteritis has resulted from moldy or musty feed. Drugs such as bismuth subnitrate, Kaolin, antibiotics, and pectin, used for diarrhea in puppies and children, may be used for rabbits.

Sore Eyes

Sore eyes are usually a symptom of a disease. The eyes themselves, however, may become sore from infection by bacteria or viruses that get into cuts and scratches; from irritation by foreign bodies; from irritation by gases; and from contaminated material getting into the eyes. Bucks' eyes may become irritated from urine. Bucks have a habit of turning quickly while urinating, allowing traces of urine to get into their eyes.

To treat sore eyes, clean them with warm salt water (1 tablespoon table salt to 1 quart warm water) or 1 percent boric acid. Nonprescription-type eye drops may also be used. Exercise and sunshine aid recovery.

Caked Udders (Caked Breast)

Caked udders, hardening of the udders due to an accumulation of fluid in the tissues, may develop just before kindling, right after

117

weaning, or at any time between kindling and weaning. The udders become hard and swollen, and are painful when touched; the breast tissue turns bright red and the ends of the teats become a darker red. The doe may refuse to allow the young to nurse because her teats are so sensitive.

This problem may occur if there are too few young in the litter to consume all the milk, or if the doe produces more milk than the young can use. To treat, apply hot towels to the udders and gently massage them. Try to remove some of the milk to relieve the pressure. If abscesses form and rupture, treat each one with an antiseptic such as tincture of iodine.

If baby rabbits are nursing, be sure that they are removing milk and that nothing is wrong with them. To help eliminate the problem of caked udders, breed a doe that produces large amounts of milk about ten days before her litter is weaned.

Sore hocks

Sore hocks have a number of causes. Many rabbits move quickly around the hutch, stamping their feet, which bruises their hocks. Constant exposure to hard floors and contact with urine may be contributing factors. If the rabbit cuts its foot on the wire of the cage, infection may set in, also causing sore hocks.

118

courtesy Dr. Karl W. Hagen

Sore hocks are very painful to a rabbit.

A mildly affected animal may be treated by cleaning the infected foot with soap and water, then applying an ointment such as iodine every other day until the sores heal. If the animal is seriously affected, it should be destroyed. Proper sanitation practices will help eliminate sore hocks. Remember: good management and good sanitation produce healthy rabbits.

119

Ear Canker

Rabbits, like all other animals, become infested with external parasites. The main parasite found outside the body is the ear mite, which is microscopic in size.

A rabbit that has ear mites shakes its head, holds its head to one side, and scratches at its

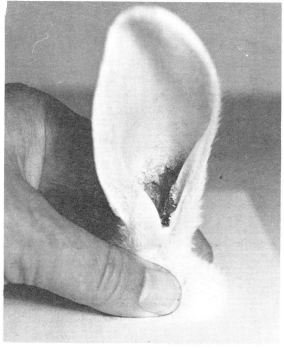

courtesy Dr. Karl W. Hagen

Ear canker.

120

ears. The ears become infected, and crusts and scabs form in them. If the condition isn't treated, crusts or scabs cover the entire inside of the ears, sometimes extending to the outside.

To treat, swab the ears and remove as much of the debris as possible, being sure to remove the scabs from the sores and the pus from the bottom of each ear. When this is done, apply a solution made of 1 part iodiform, 10 parts ether, and 25 parts olive oil with an eye-dropper, being sure that the inside of the ear and all sores or scabs are thoroughly saturated. Olive oil alone may be used if the other two products are not available.

I swab my rabbits' ears with oil at least once a week as a preventive action. Ear mites may also be controlled by using tick and flea powders that are sold for dogs and cats. First, clean the ear, then sprinkle the powder into it. When external parasites are present, good sanitation measures should be taken, such as cleaning the hutches and feeding equipment thoroughly every day.

Coccidiosis

This is a parasite disease that causes damage to both the intestinal tract and to the liver. The parasite can be seen only with a microscope. A rabbit with coccidiosis becomes listless and potbellied, and loses its appetite. Diarrhea usually occurs and pneumonia may develop. If an outbreak of this disease occurs, a veterinarian should be consulted immediately.

Try to prevent coccidiosis. Keep the hutch floors clean and dry, and remove droppings immediately. If you use all-wire floors, keeping the hutch clean is a minor problem. Prevent fecal contamination of food and water. This occurs when pans or dishes are used which allow the rabbits to get into their food.

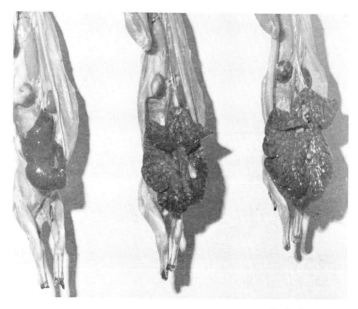

courtesy Dr. Karl W. Hagen

The rabbit on the left is free of disease; the other two are seriously affected by coccidiosis.

Heat Stroke

Heat stroke is usually a seasonal problem caused by excessive exposure to direct sunlight or by lack of adequate ventilation. The symptoms are panting, mouth hanging open, and extreme listlessness.

To treat, briefly submerge the rabbit in cold water to cool it and then place it in a shaded area with adequate ventilation. The problem may be prevented by providing shade and good air flow around the cage or hutch.

Face and Nose Scabs

Inflammation and irritation around the nose and on the face usually accompany face and nose scabs. These are caused by secretions from a runny nose, bites, external parasites, rubbing the nose with the feet, gases from dirty pens, and so on.

Antibiotic injections are very helpful in treating this condition. Medication placed around the mouth usually is licked off or rubbed off with the feet. To prevent face and nose scabs, eliminate the conditions that cause the irritation.

Buck Teeth

The large front incisor teeth should meet at an angle so that they will wear evenly. Sometimes this does not occur, and the animal has difficulty eating.

The long teeth should be cut off so that they will be even with the rest of the teeth. They may be cut with bone cutters (or many times ordinary wire cutters will be adequate) and the sharp edges filed down with an ordinary rat-tail file. Animals with buck teeth should not be used for breeding. The trait may be inherited.

Slobbers

This is another name for chronic drooling, sometimes accompanied by swollen cheeks. It may be caused by the rabbit eating excessive amounts of green feed (or in the case of young rabbits, unaccustomed green feed), sniffles, coccidiosis, or bad teeth.

Treatment will depend upon the cause. If it is too much green feed, cut down on the amount. If it is irregular feeding of green feed, give green feed daily. If it is due to bad or long teeth, correct this condition by either removing the bad teeth or cutting off the long teeth.

Abscesses

An abscess is a localized collection of pus surrounded by inflamed tissue. Abscesses often form when the skin has been broken (by a cut, a bite, or any type of an abrasion) and an infection has taken hold. They may also result from an infection that is carried from one place in the body to another by the blood stream.

To treat, open the abscess and drain it of pus; clean it thoroughly with fresh water; then apply an antiseptic such as tincture of iodine.

Mastitis

In mastitis, the udders become swollen, hot, and sore to the touch, as in caked udder. The infection travels into the udder through the teat canal. Injury and irritation from caked udder may cause mastitis.

Antibiotic injections are the best-known treatment. If abscesses form and rupture, treat them locally with an antiseptic such as tincture of iodine.

This chapter has described some of the most common diseases that appear in the average rabbitry. If a problem that has not been mentioned in this chapter occurs in your rabbitry, check the Appendix for a more complete list of symptoms, diseases, and cures. If you are unsure of what is causing the disease, consult a veterinarian who is qualified to diagnose and treat rabbit ailments.

ten
Selecting, Grooming, and Showing

As a general rule, the rabbit fancier should not raise rabbits just for show purposes. He should instead select from his herd the very best animals and enter these in shows.

Successful rabbit showing begins with the foundation stock. You can be an excellent manager and follow the best feeding program, but if your breeding stock lacks the bred-in ability to pass on desirable characteristics to offspring, your efforts will be entirely wasted.

Even though show winnings mean a lot, the production record of a rabbit means even more. If, for instance, a doe should receive first place in a show but has a history of poor production, that doe is not suitable from the meat production standpoint. Every rabbitman, whether he

127

courtesy USDA

To carry an adult rabbit, grasp the skin of the rabbit's neck and shoulders with one hand while supporting the hindquarters with the other.

128

owns one rabbit or a thousand, should consider production ability to be very important

Showing rabbits can be a lot of fun, and provides clean, wholesome competition. Of course, it is important to remember that you must be a good sport, whether you win or lose.

Condition and Performance

The show table is the place where any rabbit fancier may best observe the type of animal he is striving to breed. Perhaps a show's greatest contribution is the incentive it provides to produce better rabbits of all breeds. It affords the breeder an opportunity to evaluate his efforts by allowing comparisons with other rabbits of the same breed.

Show success depends on the rabbit's condition and the breeding program. Preparation of a show rabbit must be started in plenty of time so it will be properly developed and be in the peak of condition at judging time.

Important decisions must be made in preparing a rabbit of any breed for showing. You must select the outstanding prospects for type, breed character, and density and texture of fur. Prospects must also be of the proper age for the particular class in which they will be entered.

The correct time for beginning the conditioning of your show rabbit is before it is born, at the mating time of its parents. Mate only rabbits that are in good condition and appear to have the prospect of a show rabbit. When you select breeding stock to produce prospective show entries, choose animals that are firm of flesh and alert, with bright eyes and a smooth, clean coat. It is better to wait a few days to get your breeding stock in good condition than to mate animals that are in poor condition and get a very promising youngster only to find you cannot get it in good condition for showing.

Handle your show stock. Get them used to being handled so that they will not be frightened, and teach them to pose so they will show to the best advantage. Any show rabbit that is alert, fresh, and well trained will make an excellent appearance and impression on a judge. A few minutes a day with the rabbits you intend to show will go a long way toward taming them. Pose them daily on a table in your rabbitry.

When posing your rabbit, let it sit in a natural position. Do not stretch it out on the table. Brush the rabbit's fur each day with your hands, stroking from the head to the tail. This will remove loose hairs and give the coat a good sheen.

The condition and performance of your rabbit on the judging table will determine the honors you will win at the show. Follow the hints in this chapter, and when you produce that top show rabbit, it will go out and win the honors for you.

Show Check List

You can learn a lot about showing rabbits from observing a rabbit show in action. Here are some pointers that will help you become a winner. Though one or two have been discussed above, they have been included here so that all the pointers are together for easy reference.

1. Select your best rabbits for showing; do this early enough to get them in good condition by the time the show opens.

2. Start working with your rabbit at least six weeks before a show. Brush it with a very soft brush and rub the coat with your hands to get out the old, dead hair and give the rabbit a silky coat. This also helps gentle the rabbit. At this time you should also teach the rabbit how to sit on a table. If the rabbit jumps around on the show table, the judge will not take much time with it.

3. Read all the rules and regulations about the show so you will know whether or not your rabbit will qualify. Ear canker, sore hocks, and other irregularities will disqualify your rabbit.

4. Your rabbit should be tattooed properly for identification before you go to the show. Rabbits should be clean. Corn meal rubbed into the hair over a period of time will help take out

hutch stains. Stains should be cleaned well in advance of the show. Ears should be watched carefully for signs of canker. And look for anything else that would disqualify the rabbit so that corrective steps may be taken in plenty of time before the show.

5. When you get to the show, check your entry with the show superintendent or secretary. He will tell you where to put the rabbit after getting the necessary information from you. Usually, the exhibitor does not have to feed or care for the rabbit during the show. The show committee will take care of that. They will also take the rabbits to and from the judging table. Sometimes they ask the exhibitor to assist.

6. As the judge looks over the rabbit, he tells the secretary what to write down on the official record about the rabbit. This information is usually also written on the back of the card attached to the pen. A paper sticker showing the rabbit's placing is often placed on the front of the card.

7. If possible, the exhibitor should be present when his rabbits are being judged. There is much to learn from the judge's comments.

8. In judging and entering events, the classifications of the American Rabbit Breeders Association usually prevail. Any rabbit fancier who intends to show rabbits regularly is advised

courtesy Larry Lloyd

A champion New Zealand White doe and buck at the ARBA national convention. Judge is Guy Leger of Lake Charles, Louisiana.

to obtain a copy of the Association's official guide to determine the ages and weights of official classes. This guide also describes the requirements for a correct type of each breed, with listings of all varieties. In most shows the following classes are used: Senior Doe, Senior Buck, Intermediate Doe, Intermediate Buck, Junior Doe, Junior Buck, Pre Junior, Meat Pen, Best Opposite, and various fur classes.

133

9. Remember, it takes time to get ready for a show. Those who enter at the last minute and do not prepare their rabbits usually do not do so well.

10. Whether you win or lose, be a good sport. Try to learn everything about the type of rabbit you entered so that at the next show your chances of winning will be greatly increased.

Shipping Show Rabbits

A rabbit fancier should take advantage of the many shows outside of his immediate area. This will give him different competition and enable him to increase his knowledge about his particular breed.

When you are not able to take your rabbits to an out-of-town show, they may be shipped. This is a practice followed by many professionals, so rabbit shows are usually equipped to handle shipped animals.

The shipping container should be large so that the rabbit will be comfortable, but at the same time not too large. The rabbit should not be able to jump around. The container should be solid, with ventilation and a place for some food. Animals shipped from the Double D Rabbitry are given hay instead of the usual feed. It lasts longer and doesn't spill. Instructions for feeding and watering while in transit should be securely placed on the container, especially when the animal must be on an extended trip.

Before you enter any animal that will be shipped, always check to see how the show committee wants it shipped, by what type carrier, and when it should arrive. By following their instructions, the rabbit will be properly cared for and the show committee will know exactly when to expect the animal.

eleven
Keeping Records

A simple but complete system of record keeping is necessary in order to keep track of the daily performance of the rabbitry. Many rabbitmen, from those with just a few rabbits to those running large commercial operations, have failed because they neglected to take the time to record the progress of the rabbitry each day. Relying on the memory alone is foolish.

This chapter is designed to help the beginner set up records that will tell at a glance what is going on and what must be done each day. Illustrations of the various preprinted records available have been included.

The small rabbitry with two or three rabbits will not require a system of records other than a hutch card for each doe and buck. These cards

will tell all the information necessary to successfully take care of the animals.

The person who is interested in building up
a rabbitry that will provide a regular income
must keep more detailed records. Besides hutch
cards, records should be kept of sales of breeding stock, diseases and cures, meat sold, overall
breeding, feed purchased, equipment purchased, sales of fertilizer, plus other information
as needed. A discussion of how to handle these
items accurately and simply will be found later
in this chapter.

A proper system of records takes very little
time to keep up to date. The information the
records provide can mean extra profits for the
rabbitry.

Hutch Cards

Possibly the most important of all records
in the rabbitry is the hutch card kept for each
mature buck and doe. This card should be
mounted at the front of each rabbit's cage
where it is readily available.

A properly filled out hutch card will tell the
number of the buck or doe, date of mating, date
of kindling, number in the litter, and litter
weight at various dates before weaning. This information is necessary for the operation of a
successful rabbitry, and takes only a minute to
enter on the card. To protect this card from ad-

Keeping Records

PURINA BUCK RECORD CARD

EAR NO. _____ CAGE NO. _____

BORN _____ SIRE _____   DAM _____ WEIGHT 2 MOS. _____

DOE SERVED	DATE	LITTER SIZE	WEIGHT	JRS. SAVED Bucks	JRS. SAVED Does	DOE SERVED	DATE	LITTER SIZE	WEIGHT	JRS. SAVED Bucks	JRS. SAVED Does

SP 3157E   Printed in U.S.A.

A hutch card for the service buck.

PURINA RABBIT CAGE RECORD CARD

NAME OR EAR NO. _____   BORN _____   CAGE NO. _____

SIRE _____ DAM _____

SERVED BY	DATE	TESTED	KINDLED	NUMBER OF YOUNG BORN	LEFT	ADDED	RAISED	DIED	JRS. SAVED BUCKS	DOES	WEIGHT	REMARKS

SP 1340F   Printed in U.S.A.

A hutch card for the breeding doe.

139

verse weather conditions, place it inside a clear plastic bag.

Hutch cards for both does and bucks may be purchased from a number of rabbit supply houses. Most feed companies provide sizable quantities upon request at no charge. Although these free cards carry the company advertisement, they fill all the requirements for an excellent hutch card. A list of feed companies that furnish these cards is found in the Appendix

A hutch card for a breeding doe is shown on page 139. Constant checking on the weight of a litter is necessary in order to determine whether the young are receiving enough milk and are developing correctly.

Weigh the litter one or two days after birth. If this is done quietly and gently, the doe will not object. A litter of seven young should weigh about a pound. Weigh the litter again at three weeks and at eight weeks. The final weight should be entered on the hutch card and the breeding chart of both doe and buck. When it is necessary to foster young to another mother, this information should be entered on the hutch card for future reference.

A card for a breeding buck is shown on page 139. Note that the buck's participation in the breeding process can be determined quickly. A rabbitman can tell at a glance whether the buck is being used for service on a regular basis and if he sires large litters. Properly filled out hutch cards can tell the entire history of the rabbitry at a glance.

Performance Records

As the rabbitry grows in size, another set of records should be kept. These are called performance records; they contain all the data usually kept on the individual hutch card plus information about the rabbit's ancestors. This information is invaluable when you want to determine the characteristics of potential offspring (for example, high producers can be mated to others showing the same characteristic).

Performance records are also valuable when the hutch card is lost or destroyed, as sometimes happens when the rabbit pulls it from the holder and eats it. With this second set of records, a new card can easily be filled out.

Another advantage in keeping these records is that they enable the rabbitman to cull the animals which kindle small litters, are continuously underweight, destroy their young, and have other bad traits.

Keeping performance records up to date may take a few extra minutes each day, but this information could determine the success or failure of your rabbitry.

HOW TO RAISE RABBITS FOR FUN AND PROFIT

PURINA BUCK PERFORMANCE RECORD SHEET

NAME _____ EAR NO. _____ HUTCH NO. _____

BORN _____ WEIGHT _____ QUALITY
- Head & Ears _____
- Type _____
- Fur _____
- Bone _____

DISPOSITION _____ DATE _____

LITTER RECORD											
Doe Served	Date	Litter Size	Weight	Jrs. Saved Bucks	Does	Doe Served	Date	Litter Size	Weight	Jrs. Saved Bucks	Does

SIRE

Name _____
No. _____
R.O.P. _____
- Sire _____ No. _____
  - R.O.P. _____
    - Sire _____ No. _____
    - Dam _____ No. _____
- Dam _____ No. _____
  - R.O.P. _____
    - Sire _____ No. _____
    - Dam _____ No. _____

DAM

Name _____
No. _____
R.O.P. _____
- Sire _____ No. _____
  - R.O.P. _____
    - Sire _____ No. _____
    - Dam _____ No. _____
- Dam _____ No. _____
  - R.O.P. _____
    - Sire _____ No. _____
    - Dam _____ No. _____

SP 6357A-7-63

Printed in U.S.A.

The buck performance record sheet.

142

PURINA DOE PERFORMANCE RECORD

NAME _____ EAR NO. _____ HUTCH NO. _____

BORN _____ WEIGHT _____ QUALITY

Head & Ears _____
Type _____
Fur _____
Bone _____

DISPOSITION _____ DATE _____

LITTER RECORD

SERVED BY	DATE	TESTED	DATE KINDLED	NUMBER OF YOUNG					JRS. SAVED		WEIGHT	LBS. SOLD	INCOME
				BORN	LEFT	ADDED	RAISED	DIED	BUCKS	DOES			

POUNDS PRODUCED: 1st YEAR _____ 2nd YEAR _____ 3rd YEAR _____

INCOME: 1st YEAR _____ 2nd YEAR _____ 3rd YEAR _____ TOTAL _____

SIRE
NAME _____ NO. _____ R.O.P. _____
SIRE _____ NO. _____ R.O.P. _____
DAM _____ NO. _____ R.O.P. _____
SIRE _____ NO. _____ DAM _____ NO. _____
SIRE _____ NO. _____ DAM _____ NO. _____

DAM
NAME _____ NO. _____ R.O.P. _____
SIRE _____ NO. _____ R.O.P. _____
DAM _____ NO. _____ R.O.P. _____
SIRE _____ NO. _____ DAM _____ NO. _____
SIRE _____ NO. _____ DAM _____ NO. _____

SP 1201A

Printed in U. S. A.

The doe performance record sheet.

143

Financial Records

The financial records of a rabbitry tell one of two things: profit or loss. These records may be set up very simply using a small bound journal available at any office supply store.

All income from selling rabbits and their products, fertilizer, and breeding stock is entered on a page titled "Income." On the "Expense" page, the cost of such items as feed, equipment and supplies, advertising, and licenses should be entered. At the end of each month, both pages are added up and the answer will be either a profit or a loss. There are other items such as depreciation, value of breeding stock, and prorating of utilities, but these are disregarded here because the beginner is trying to start a small rabbitry, not a multilevel corporation.

No attempt will be made here to teach elementary bookkeeping. The best way to learn what should be kept in the financial records of the rabbitry would be to purchase a simple how-to-do-it book on bookkeeping. These books are available in most bookstores, office supply stores, and department stores.

Licenses

Before you invest money in rabbits, equipment, and other supplies, determine whether you need a license to begin a rabbitry. Some areas require city, county, and state occupational licenses, health department permits, and sales tax certificates. Many areas of the country carry restrictive ordinances that forbid such a venture as a rabbitry.

In some states, such as Florida, rabbit raising is considered an agricultural venture and no license is required. Health department permits are needed, however. Also, check any restrictions placed on the property where the rabbitry is located, since there is always the possibility that years before the property had restrictions placed on it that forbid such a business. If licenses are required, you may have to keep a complete set of books on the rabbitry since the cost of the license is sometimes determined by the net profit.

Consult a local lawyer before investing more than a hundred dollars in a rabbitry. He will be able to advise you on what you must have in the way of licenses, permits, and financial records. The small cost of his advice could save you many dollars in the future.

Pedigree

A pedigree is a genealogical record of the rabbit. A rabbit of a certain breed is usually considered pedigreed when its parentage can be proven for three generations back, and it has the

CERTIFICATE OF SALE

PEDIGREE

BRED BY.

PURCHASED FROM. Double D

RABBITRY ___ DATE 8-10-72

BREED— California

CONDITION EXCELLENT

DEFECTS IF ANY NONE

DIET PELLETS

NAME Double D 721-H

EAR MARK H-217 WT. 9 COLOR WH

REG. No.

WINNINGS:

SIRE Double D T21 WT. 9½

EAR MARK 42-H COLOR WH

REG. No.

WINNINGS:

SIRE Double D T62 WT. 9

EAR MARK 681 COLOR WH

REG. No.

WINNINGS: CHAMPION

SIRE Double D 6-10-5 WT. 9½

EAR MARK 98-76 COLOR WH

REG. No.

DAM JAMS DH417 WT. 9

EAR MARK X217 COLOR WH

REG. No.

DAM Double D H14 WT. 10

EAR MARK 71 COLOR WH

REG. No.

WINNINGS:

SIRE SIMPSON V-6124 WT. 10

EAR MARK HA1 COLOR WH

REG. No.

DAM Double D 7-11-4 WT. 9½

EAR MARK Z21 COLOR WH

REG. No.

DAM Double D H29 WT. 9½

EAR MARK 76-HA COLOR WH

REG. No.

WINNINGS: 2nd place

SIRE Double D T75 WT. 10½

EAR MARK 692 COLOR WH

REG. No.

WINNINGS: BEST OF SHOW

SIRE Double D 2-1-29 WT. 9

EAR MARK H491 COLOR WH

REG. No.

DAM HOWAD S-421 WT. 9½

EAR MARK BB21 COLOR WH

REG. No.

DAM Double D H418 WT. 9

EAR MARK H-21 COLOR WH

REG. No.

WINNINGS:

SIRE J+M 2691 WT. 9½

EAR MARK N-72 COLOR WH

REG. No.

DAM Double D 6-20-1 WT. 10

EAR MARK 9861 COLOR WH

REG. No.

MASTER MIX

This is to certify that I have this day sold the above to

_____and that its pedigree is correct

to the best of my knowledge and belief.

Date_____ Signed_____

OTHER INFORMATION:—

A properly filled out pedigree. These pedigree forms are

outward appearance (color, eyes, type of coat, and so on) plus the physical features (body structure, correct hips, erectness of ears, and so on) of the breed as listed in the Standard of Perfection of the American Rabbit Breeders Association. When this information is satisfactory, a pedigree may be issued.

Any rabbit fancier can make out the pedigree on his own, but he would be smart to double check all his information before doing so. The rabbit fancier should remember that his reputation goes with the pedigree. It is in fact an advertisement for himself and his rabbitry.

Another reason the rabbit fancier or breeder should be a member of the ARBA is that rabbitmen looking for new stock will be quicker to buy stock from an ARBA member than from a nonmember. ARBA membership does not guarantee good stock, however, nor is it required of a professional rabbitman. As in other hobbies and professions, membership in a national association gives assistance, provides opportunities for meetings and friendships with other breeders, and gives an air of respectability to the rabbitman and his rabbitry.

Pedigree forms are available from a number of sources. They may be purchased from the ARBA, and at least one feed company will provide them at no charge. Here again, refer to the Appendix for sources. A properly filled out pedigree form is shown on page 146.

Registration

Registration of a rabbit certifies that it is high-quality stock, it meets the requirements set forth in the Standard of Perfection, and it is an excellent specimen of that particular breed. The rabbit that has a pedigree showing that its forebears were registered will be of very high quality. It will be likely to produce perfect off-spring and will command a high price when sold for breeding stock.

Registration must be done by a certified registrar of the ARBA, who is impartial and approves only a top-quality rabbit. For more information about registering rabbits, contact the ARBA or check the listings in various rabbit magazines of the certified judges. There will be a fee for registering your rabbit.

Tattooing

All the rabbits that you intend to keep should be tattooed. This is a permanent marking method that does not disfigure or injure the rabbit and is recognized by the ARBA. It is required when exhibiting rabbits in fairs or rabbit shows.

Tattooing instruments may be purchased from most livestock supply houses, or they may

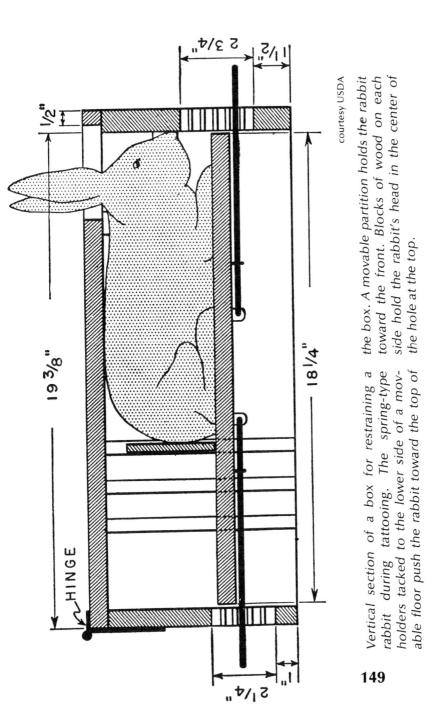

Vertical section of a box for restraining a rabbit during tattooing. The spring-type holders tacked to the lower side of a movable floor push the rabbit toward the top of the box. A movable partition holds the rabbit toward the front. Blocks of wood on each side hold the rabbit's head in the center of the hole at the top.

be obtained from many of the advertisers in rabbit magazines. For the large rabbitry, the commercial tattoo is recommended, since it places the necessary combination of letters and numbers in the rabbit's ear at one time.

If you have only a handful of rabbits, however, a simple method may be used that will do the job satisfactorily. This method calls for a straight pin and some India ink. Prick the skin inside the left ear in the form of the desired mark. Then apply India ink to the prick marks. This method is time consuming, but if you are patient, the results will be good and the rabbit will experience only minor discomfort.

To successfully tattoo a rabbit, you must restrain it so that your hands are free to do the actual work. The rabbit will become nervous and may kick violently. One quick kick by a disturbed rabbit can leave you with deep, long, and very painful wounds.

A tattoo box is effective in restraining a rabbit, and it's easy to build. The general layout of a typical tattoo box is shown on page 149. Basically, it is a closed box with a top that can be removed and an opening for the rabbit's ears. The inside should have a movable partition so that slight pressure may be placed on the rabbit to keep it restrained.

Rabbits to be sold for fryers or inferior stock to be sold for pets should not be tattooed.

A rule of thumb is to tattoo all stock being kept for breeders. Remember, the number you put on that ear is permanent; it is an advertisement for your rabbitry. The number or letter should always be placed in the left ear so that if the rabbit is pedigreed stock and is to be registered with the ARBA the registration number may be placed in the right ear as required.

The number or letter combination placed in the left ear is determined by the owner himself. Some rabbitries use a letter and a number, such as D-1, for doe number one. Others use a number combination such as 73-32, for 1973, rabbit number thirty-two. The beginning rabbitman should keep the numbering system simple so that as the rabbitry expands the numbering system can expand. When a rabbit is acquired that already carries a number, that number should not be changed. The new owner uses that number as his own.

twelve

Processing for Market

Rabbits may be disposed of in four ways: they may be sold alive to the processor who does the slaughtering; they may be processed for direct sale; they may be processed for home use; or they may be sold for breeders or as pets. The beginning rabbitman should go into the project of rabbit raising with the idea of selling the rabbits for meat or pets rather than for breeding, as the breeding market is limited.

Crating and Transporting Live Rabbits

Most rabbits are sent to market alive. Rabbits in good condition, properly crated, can be transported with safety. But they should not be exposed to extremely hot or cold conditions. Good ventilation is important. Avoid overcrowding. Although it is better to have individual shipping compartments, it will be more practical for the beginner who is transporting rabbits for relatively short distances to use shipping crates made from packing boxes. As the project grows and there are many rabbits to market at one time, more permanent shipping crates should be provided.

Slaughtering and Skinning

The beginning rabbitman should learn how to prepare rabbits for market and home use. The person who can dress and package rabbit meat attractively will help build the market.

Slaughtering for market should be done in a clean, sanitary place free from dust and flies. Fasten a board, 2 feet long, 6 inches wide, and 3/4 inch thick, to a wall as you would a shelf. On the outer edge, 8 to 10 inches apart, put two small meat hooks to hang the rabbit on. Provide some type of container on the floor beneath the shelf to catch the blood, head, and entrails. Running water should be available. Be sure to check with your county health department about local slaughtering regulations before you begin.

A beginner would profit by visiting a rabbit slaughtering plant before undertaking slaughtering on a large scale; however, the work is generally done in the following manner.

Stun the rabbit by a heavy blow at the base of the skull (behind the ears) and hang it up by inserting the hooks between the tendon and bone of the hind legs, just above the hock. (Some processors hang the rabbit up by one leg only. Either way is satisfactory.)

Cut the head off and let the rabbit bleed thoroughly so that the meat will have a good color. Do not let blood get on the pelt.

Remove the tail and cut off the front feet. Then cut the skin just below the hocks and open it on the inside of the leg to the base of the tail. Loosen the skin around the hind legs and peel the fur down over the legs, hindquarters, and body. Take particular care to not get hair on the carcass.

After the skin is removed, cut open the carcass down the middle of the abdomen, starting near the tail and ending at the neck. Do not puncture the entrails. Remove the entrails, leaving the liver in place. Remove the gall bladder. Cut the hind legs off at the hock joint.

Rinse the carcass in cold water to remove hair and blood and also to clean the carcass. Rinse the neck thoroughly to remove any blood. Do not leave the carcass in water more than 15 minutes for it will absorb water.

Chill the carcasses overnight before cutting them up. Rabbits should be cut according to the requirements of the market. The various cuts of

155

Method of killing a rabbit by breaking its neck.

Various cuts of rabbit meat.

rabbit are shown on page 156. Try to have a finished product that is thoroughly clean and attractive.

Another method of killing a rabbit is shown on page 156. This is not recommended for the beginner, however. Hold the animal by its hind legs with your left hand. Place the thumb of your right hand on the neck just back of the ears, with four fingers extended under the rabbit's chin. Push down on the neck with your right hand, stretching the animal. Press down with the thumb. Then raise the animal's head with a quick movement and dislocate its neck. The animal becomes unconscious and ceases to struggle. This method is instantaneous and painless when done correctly.

Preparation of the Pelt

As soon as the pelt has been removed from the carcass, it should be stretched for drying. Wet skins left in a pile for a long period of time become "burned," causing the fur to loosen from the pelt.

Use a good spring-steel stretcher. The skin should be inside out—that is, with the fur on the inside. Draw it down over the stretcher with the front legs centered on one side between the arms of the stretcher. Stretch the skin downward as far as possible. Fasten the skin of each hind leg to an arm of the stretcher with a clothespin.

157

Fur that laps over the wet part of the skin, and folds or wrinkles in the skin, provide places for flies to lay their eggs, making a good skin almost worthless.

The skin should be hung to dry in a well-ventilated place away from artificial heat and direct sun. When it is thoroughly dry it may be stored. If skins are to be kept for any length of time they should be sprinkled with naphthalene flakes or moth crystals.

Skins may be kept in good condition for many months if they are wrapped in newspapers, so that two skins do not come in contact with each other, and put in a dry, airtight container, free from moths and flies.

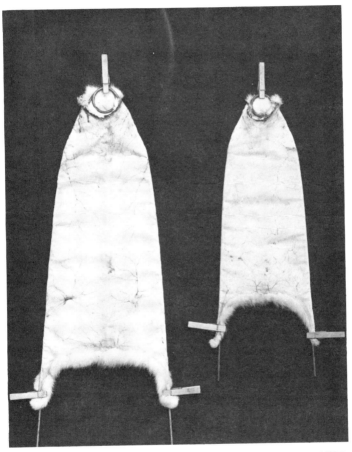

courtesy USDA

Properly stretched pelts.

thirteen
By-Products: Making the Rabbitry Pay

There are many ways to make money raising rabbits. The beginning rabbitman should keep in mind, however, that there is no possibility of enough income from a small rabbitry to provide a living. It is possible, though to sell enough to pay for feed and more breeding stock. As the rabbitry becomes larger, it is only natural that there will be more income.

Let's look at some of the ways to make money.

Rabbit Meat

I have already covered processing the meat for market in another chapter. After investigating the local market and checking on area laws, you may be able to begin to sell fresh meat. By providing clean, well-packaged meat, a good local trade can be developed. Word of mouth advertising is a sure-fire means of letting the neighborhood know of your project.

Rabbit Pelts

Although a small rabbitry will not have enough pelts to sell commercially, there is usually a very good local market for clean pelts. I am referring to Boy Scouts or Cub Scouts, who often use fur in the costumes they make for their Indian dances. Check with these boys, establish a fair price, and you'll have a market for the pelts after you have eaten or sold the meat.

The entire body of the rabbit—fur, meat, entrails, and feet—may be profitably used when the animal is killed. The meat may be eaten, the pelts used for garments and trimming, the feet fashioned into lucky charms, and the entrails used as pet food.

Laboratory Rabbits

If you live near a university, college, or laboratory, investigate selling your young rabbits to them. Usually they require that the rabbits be perfectly formed, of a certain weight and age, and in excellent health. Also, you will probably be expected to provide a certain number on a regular basis.

Breeding Stock

Breeding stock may be sold to others who wish to begin or to develop their rabbitry. One advantage of purchasing pedigreed animals when you start is that later on you will be able to sell the pedigreed offspring for breeding.

The sale of breeding stock is very profitable; a two-month-old fryer will bring about $1.25, while a two-month-old animal sold as a breeder will bring about $4.00. Only the best should be sold as breeders. The rest may be sold as either pets or fryers.

If you decide to sell breeding animals, the best places to advertise are local rabbit clubs and the rabbit magazines. If you advertise in magazines, however, you will have to provide shipping containers and other items needed to move a rabbit from one part of the country to another.

Worm Beds

Raising fishing worms under the rabbit hutches is another profitable enterprise. All that is required is some type of box or container the size of the outside measurements of the hutch. Place the box on the ground under the hutch so that the manure and urine fall into it.

Cultures of worms may be purchased through rabbit magazines, and if you follow the

163

instructions you will be on your way. As long as the manure is kept wet, the worms will grow. A container of eighteen to twenty-four worms brings a price in some areas of from 60 to 75 cents. And there is no work to this operation.

Fertilizer

Selling rabbit manure as garden fertilizer is also profitable. Rabbit manure is the only animal manure that will not burn a garden. It may be immediately taken from the hutch and placed on the plants.

A bushel of clean manure will bring any-where from 50 cents to $1.00. The manure at the Double D Rabbitry is not sold; it is all used for our own farm crops and flowers. A small adver-tisement in your local newspaper will probably bring all the sales you can handle.

Pets

Selling rabbits for pets accounts for about half of the rabbit production in the United States each year. Although many rabbitmen re-fuse to sell their rabbits for pets, I see no harm in it. An eight-week-old rabbit will bring from $1.50 to $2.00 as a pet. Remember that sick, deformed, or undersize rabbits must never be sold as pets.

When I sell a rabbit for a pet I always give one of the excellent booklets put out by feed companies to the new owner. This enables him or her to learn something about the rabbit and insures better care for the new pet. I also provide a small plastic bag containing a two or three day supply of feed and explain what the rabbit needs and how it should be handled. This increases the probability that the rabbit will survive and also that the new owner will come back for more rabbits!

fourteen
Let's Eat Rabbit

Rabbit meat may be prepared and served in many attractive ways. In fact, rabbit meat can be substituted for chicken in most recipes with successful and satisfying results.

There is no dark meat on a rabbit. The meat is fine grained, with a mild but delicious flavor. It is suitable not only for unrestricted diets but also for diets requiring high protein and low fat content. Rabbit meat is an excellent addition to the reducing diet.

In comparing a rabbit with a chicken of comparable size, you will note that there is more meat on the rabbit carcass than on the chicken. Also, the cooked meat may be removed with greater ease from the rabbit.

The following recipes are typical of the many that may be used. All have proven successful, and of course variations are limited only by the imagination of the cook.

Good Eating!

Rabbit Salad Loaf

1 envelope unflavored gelatin
1/4 cup cold water
1 2/3 cups hot rabbit broth
Salt, as desired
1 teaspoon grated onion or onion juice
1 1/2 tablespoons vinegar or lemon juice
1 hard cooked egg, sliced
6 stuffed olives, sliced
1 1/2 cups cooked rabbit, diced
1/3 cup cooked peas
3 tablespoons celery, finely chopped

Soften the gelatin in the cold water a few minutes and dissolve it in the hot broth. Add salt, onion, and lemon juice. Pour a layer of the gelatin mixture 1/4 inch deep in the bottom of an oiled 3 or 4 cup loaf pan or mold. Cool until firm. Allow the rest of the gelatin mixture to thicken but not set.

Press a design of the sliced egg and olives lightly into the firm gelatin in the pan.

Add the rabbit, peas, and celery to the thickened gelatin broth mixture, and pour it

carefully over the sliced egg and olives. Chill until firm. Unmold and slice for serving.
(courtesy USDA)

Rabbit Salad

2 to 3 pound rabbit, cut in serving pieces
1 1/2 cups celery, diced
1/2 cup sweet pickle, diced
1/4 teaspoon monosodium glutamate (optional)
1/2 cup mayonnaise
2 tablespoons lemon juice
1 teaspoon salt
1/8 teaspoon pepper

Place the rabbit pieces in a stew pan, cover with boiling water, and season with salt and pepper. Cover and simmer 1 or 2 hours until tender. Drain and cool, saving the broth for gravy. Remove the meat from the bones and dice. Combine the diced rabbit meat, celery, and pickles, and mix with remaining ingredients. Chill thoroughly and serve on crisp lettuce leaves with a garnish of hard cooked egg.

Rabbit Pot Pie

2 to 3 pound rabbit
Celery tops
1 teaspoon salt
1/4 teaspoon pepper
3 tablespoons margarine

3 tablespoons onion, chopped
1/2 cup green pepper, diced
3 tablespoons flour
1/2 cup celery, sliced
1/2 teaspoon monosodium glutamate (optional)
2 tablespoons pimiento, chopped
1/2 recipe for pie crust

Place the rabbit pieces and celery tops in a stew pan and cover with boiling water. Season with salt and pepper. Cover and simmer 1 to 2 hours until tender. Drain and cool, saving the broth for gravy. Remove the meat from the bones and dice. Saute the onion, green pepper, and celery in margarine. Remove from heat and blend in flour, salt, and monosodium glutamate. Add 3 cups of broth, stirring constantly. Add rabbit meat and pimiento and heat well. Put into a casserole. Top the hot mixture with crust made from half a standard recipe. Bake at 450° for 15 minutes or until the crust browns.

Braised Rabbit With Gravy
2 to 3 pound rabbit, cut in serving pieces
Flour, salt, pepper
3 tablespoons cooking oil
1/4 cup hot water
2 tablespoons flour
2 cups milk

Roll rabbit in a mixture of flour, salt, and

pepper. Heat the oil in a heavy fry pan and brown the rabbit slowly, turning it to brown all sides. Add water and cover pan tightly.

Reduce heat and cook slowly until meat is tender (about 1 hour), adding a little more water if needed. Uncover and cook 5 minutes longer to recrisp the meat. Remove the rabbit from the pan and keep it hot.

Remove all but 2 tablespoons of fat from the pan. Stir in the 2 tablespoons flour. Cook until mixture bubbles. Add milk slowly, stirring constantly. Cook until thick, stirring occasionally, then cook a little longer. Add salt and pepper if needed.
(courtesy USDA)

Rabbit in Barbecue Sauce
2 to 3 pound rabbit, cut in serving pieces
Flour
Salt
Pepper
3 tablespoons cooking oil
Barbecue sauce

Roll rabbit in a mixture of flour, salt, and pepper. Heat the oil and brown the rabbit on all sides over moderate heat (about 20 minutes). Pour the barbecue sauce over the rabbit and cover the pan.

Bake at 325° (slow oven) about 45 minutes,

or until the meat is tender. Uncover the pan and place under broiler. Broil 15 minutes, or until the meat is brown.
(courtesy USDA)

Stewed Rabbit
3 to 4 pound rabbit, cut into serving pieces
1 1/2 teaspoons salt
Hot water

Put the rabbit into a pan large enough to hold the pieces without crowding. Season with salt and add enough water to half cover the rabbit. Cover the pan and cook over low heat about 1 1/2 hours, or until the meat is very tender. Add more water during cooking if needed.

Serve hot with gravy made by thickening the broth and seasoning as desired, or use the meat and broth in other recipes.
(courtesy USDA)

Rabbit Chop Suey
2 cups cooked rabbit meat, coarsely cut
1/4 cup sliced mushrooms
2 tablespoons butter
1 cup celery, thinly sliced
1 small carrot, cut in thin strips
1 medium onion, thinly sliced
1 1/2 cups rabbit broth
2 cups canned bean sprouts, with liquid

3 tablespoons cornstarch
3 tablespoons soy sauce
Salt and pepper, as desired
1 1/2 cups hot cooked rice

Cook rabbit meat and mushrooms in butter over low heat until lightly browned. Add celery, carrot, onion, and broth.

Cover the pan and boil gently 10 to 15 minutes, or until vegetables are tender. Add the bean sprouts and liquid, and heat to boiling.

Mix the cornstarch and soy sauce; add gradually to the boiling mixture, stirring constantly. Cook 2 minutes, or until slightly thickened. Add salt and pepper. Serve over rice. (courtesy USDA)

Curried Rabbit

2 cups rabbit broth
1/4 cup onion, finely chopped
1 clove garlic, cut in half
1 teaspoon curry powder
1/4 cup milk
1/3 cup sifted flour
2 cups cooked rabbit meat, coarsely cut
Salt and pepper, as desired
1 1/2 cups hot cooked rice

Boil broth, onion, garlic, and curry powder in a covered pan for 20 minutes. Remove garlic.

Stir the milk into the flour. Add a few tablespoons of the hot broth and stir. Add the mixture to the rest of the broth. Cook over low heat until thick and smooth. Stir frequently.

Add the rabbit meat, and salt and pepper to taste. Heat thoroughly and serve over rice. (courtesy USDA)

Rabbit Sandwich Spread
1 cup cooked rabbit meat, finely chopped
2 tablespoons onion, finely chopped
2 tablespoons green pepper, finely chopped
1/4 cup celery, finely chopped
1/4 cup sweet pickle or pickle relish, finely chopped
1/3 cup mayonnaise or salad dressing
Salt to taste

Mix all ingredients well. Keep cold. Makes 1 1/2 cups, enough for 6 sandwiches. (courtesy USDA)

Rabbit and Onions
12 small white onions
2 cups cider
1 tablespoon vinegar
1/2 cup plus 3 tablespoons flour
2 1/2 teaspoons salt
1 teaspoon celery salt
2 teaspoons paprika
1/2 teaspoon pepper
1 rabbit (2 to 3 pounds), cut in serving pieces
1/2 cup butter
1/4 cup green pepper, chopped

1/8 teaspoon garlic powder
1/2 cup ripe olives, slivered
Cook the onions in cider and vinegar 30 to 40 minutes or until tender. Combine 1/2 cup flour, salt, celery salt, paprika, and pepper. Roll rabbit pieces in flour mixture. Brown well in butter. Remove to a large saucepan or casserole. Cook green pepper and garlic powder in butter until tender. Add to rabbit with olives, onions, and cider. Cover. Cook over low heat 40 minutes or until the rabbit is tender. Remove the rabbit pieces and keep hot. Combine 3 tablespoons flour with a little cold water to form a smooth paste. Blend into pan liquid.

Rabbit a la King

2 cups cooked rabbit meat, coarsely cut
1/3 cup celery, chopped
3 tablespoons onion, finely chopped
3 tablespoons green pepper, finely chopped
3 tablespoons mushrooms, sliced
1/3 cup water
1/4 cup butter or margarine
1/4 cup sifted flour
2 1/2 cups milk
Salt and pepper, as desired
Cook the vegetables and mushrooms gently in 1/3 cup water in a covered pan until just tender. Drain and save the liquid. Melt the butter or margarine, and blend in the flour. Add

cooking liquid to milk and pour gradually into the fat-flour mixture, stirring frequently, until thick and smooth. Season.

Add vegetables, mushrooms, and rabbit meat to the sauce and heat thoroughly.

Fried Rabbit

Young rabbit, 3 pounds or less, cut into serving pieces
Flour, salt, pepper
Cooking oil

Roll the rabbit pieces in a mixture of flour, salt, and pepper. Heat oil (about 1/4 inch deep) in a heavy fry pan large enough to hold the pieces of meat without crowding. Use moderate heat for frying. Put in the large meaty pieces of rabbit first and cook about 10 minutes before adding the smaller pieces and the giblets. Turn the pieces often for even cooking, and cook until well browned and tender (about 30 minutes).

(courtesy USDA)

Creole Rabbit

3 pound rabbit, cut into serving pieces
1/4 cup milk
Flour, salt, pepper
3 tablespoons cooking oil
Creole sauce (see recipe that follows)

Dip rabbit in milk and roll it in a mixture of flour, salt, and pepper. Heat the oil, brown the rabbit on all sides, and put it in a baking dish. Pour sauce over the rabbit; cover. Bake at 325° (slow oven) 1 1/2 hours, or until the meat is tender. Uncover and bake 30 minutes longer to brown the top.
(courtesy USDA)

Creole Sauce
2 medium onions, sliced
1 clove garlic, finely chopped
1 tablespoon parsley, chopped
3 tablespoons butter, margarine, or oil
3 1/2 cups tomato juice
1/4 teaspoon Worcestershire sauce
Salt and pepper, as desired
Cook onions, garlic, and parsley in the oil until onion is golden brown. Add other ingredients (except salt and pepper) and cook gently for 15 minutes. Season to taste.
(courtesy USDA)

Baked Rabbit Hash
2 cups cooked rabbit meat, finely chopped
2 cups raw potatoes, finely chopped
2 tablespoons green pepper, chopped
3/4 cup onion, finely chopped
1 1/2 teaspoons salt

Pepper, to taste
1/2 cup rabbit broth
1/4 cup fine dry bread crumbs, mixed with margarine

Mix all the ingredients together except the crumbs. Pile lightly into a greased baking dish or pan. Cover and bake at 350° (moderate oven) about 40 minutes.

Remove cover and sprinkle crumbs over the hash. Bake uncovered 20 minutes longer to brown.
(courtesy USDA)

Hasenpfeffer

1/2 cup vinegar
2 cups water
2 teaspoons salt
Pepper, as desired
1/4 teaspoon whole cloves
2 teaspoons sugar
4 bay leaves
1 medium onion, sliced
2 to 3 pound rabbit with giblets, cut in serving pieces
Flour
3 tablespoons fat
2 teaspoons Worcestershire sauce
3 tablespoons flour

Make a pickling mixture by combining the vinegar, water, salt, pepper, cloves, sugar, bay leaves, and onion in a bowl. Add pieces of rabbit and sliced giblets and cover the bowl. Let stand in refrigerator 8 to 12 hours, turning the pieces occasionally so that they will absorb the flavor evenly.

Remove the rabbit pieces. Save the liquid and onions but discard bay leaves and cloves. Roll rabbit in flour. Heat oil in a heavy pan and brown the rabbit, turning it to brown the sides evenly.

Pour the pickling mixture over the rabbit. Cover the pan and cook over low heat about 1 hour, or until the rabbit is tender.

Put the rabbit on a platter and keep it hot. Add Worcestershire sauce to the liquid in the pan. Mix the 3 tablespoons flour with a little water; add a few tablespoons of the hot liquid to it, and pour the mixture back into the pan. Stir and cook until the sauce is thick and smooth, then cook a little longer. Pour the sauce over rabbit.

fifteen
Do's and Don'ts

By the time you reach this chapter, you've read thousands of words; you've digested some and been confused by many. Although all of the information in this book is important to the rabbit raiser and should be followed for the best possible results, here are some basic do's and don'ts which may be used as a check list.

DO'S

1. Keep feed and water clean; disease may easily be spread by contaminated food and water.

2. Clean and disinfect the nest box after each litter. Newborn rabbits are extremely susceptible to disease, and an infected

nest box may cause any number of problems.

3. Learn to recognize rabbit diseases and the proper cures. If unsure, eliminate error by calling a veterinarian.

4. Isolate all rabbits coming into the rabbitry, including those returning from rabbit shows and fairs.

5. Use all-wire cages if possible to keep the rabbit out of contact with urine and droppings. This will help eliminate sore hocks and urine burn.

6. Sear all hutch wire with a small blowtorch after a litter has been removed from a cage. The few minutes this takes are worth spending to insure the health of the next rabbit and litter that occupy the cage.

7. Always select disease-free and disease-resistant animals. There are no bargains in good breeding animals. Look at other rabbits from the same litter and at related rabbits. From these you can determine much about fur, weight, overall appearance, and other factors that go into making up a good specimen.

8. Keep water crocks clean.

9. Furnish fresh water every day.

10. Keep hutches clean and in good repair. No matter what type cage or hutch you use, it can be kept clean.

11. Try to have one buck for every eight to ten does.

12. Keep salt in front of each rabbit at all times.

13. If any rabbit becomes too fat, cut down on its ration.

14. If any rabbit does not gain weight at the proper rate, give it additional feed. At times one or two of a litter (particularly a young litter) will be pushed out by the others. If placing additional feed in the hutch does not solve the problem, remove the underfed rabbits and place them where they will be able to get the proper ration.

15. Watch carefully for ear mites. A good sign of ear canker is when the rabbit pulls its ear down and scratches it. Ear canker is painful to the rabbit and will spread quickly in the rabbitry.

16. Provide ample shade and good ventilation for your rabbitry. Direct sunlight will cause problems.

17. Place a nest box in the hutch three or four days before the doe is due to kindle.

18. Join a local rabbit club and the American Rabbit Breeders Association. Not only will you make many friends but you will gain from listening to the problems and the successes of others. This will give you ideas for improving your rabbitry.

19. Watch your animals for sore hocks, which are extremely painful.

20. Always lift a rabbit by the fold of skin behind the neck and over the shoulders, while supporting the hindquarters with your other hand.

21. Always feed and water on a regular schedule.

22. Always take the doe to the buck's cage for mating.

23. Wean fryer litters at eight weeks of age, or sooner if they come up to weight before then.

24. If you want to sell pelts, be sure that they are kept clean, well stretched, and attractive.

25. Give your rabbits lots of love. They will repay you for it.

DON'TS

1. Don't feed moldy or dirty food.

2. Do not move the rabbits from one cage to another without completely cleaning and disinfecting the new cage.

3. Do not bring a new rabbit into the rabbitry immediately. Isolate it for a period of time.

4. Allow no visitors in the rabbitry, especially rabbit breeders who could carry disease.

5. Do not purchase rabbits that have a record of low production and loss of young.

6. Rabbits in poor health should not be bred.

7. Young does should not be bred before they are ready.

8. Do not use a buck for mating more than three times a week as a general rule.

9. Do not overfeed your herd.

10. Never attempt to treat a disease unless you are sure of its cause. If in doubt, call a veterinarian.

11. Never use a buck under six months of age for mating.

12. Do not let any rabbit become overly fat. Chances of successful breeding of fat rabbits are slim.

13. Do not change brands of feed abruptly.

14. Dogs and cats should not be allowed around the rabbitry.

15. Do not leave feed sacks open.

16. Never overbreed your does. Four litters a year are sufficient for one doe.

17. Do not keep rabbits in direct sunlight.

18. Do not allow manure to pile up in the hutches.

19. Never handle sick animals at the same time you handle well ones.

20. Do not use disinfecting solutions that have become dirty.

Appendix

Common Ailments and Their Treatment

Name of Disease	External Symptoms	Internal Lesions	Cause	Prevention	Treatment
Coccidiosis	Listless, anemia, pot bellied, thin, loss of appetite, diarrhea.	White spotted liver, liver enlarged, inflamed intestine with occasional heavy mucus.	A protozoa—5 species of coccidia (Emira stiedea, etc.)	Use wire floored pens—Keep pens clean. Prevent fecal contamination of feed and water.	Feed Rapid Ade for 7 full days, Rabbit Family 4 days, Rapid Ade 1 day. Rabbit Family 4 days and a final day of Rapid Ade. Clean and disinfect pans.
Ear mites mange	Scabs in ears, scratches head, may lose weight.	Scabs or crust in ear. Mites can be seen with microscope.	Ear mite.	Prevent contact with affected individuals.	Clean ear with cotton swab and apply weekly for 4 weeks 5% phenol in sweet oil or 5% chlordane solution.

Enteritis non-specific	Scours—dirty behind, feces dark, poorly formed, may stick to wire.	Inflamed intestines—feces in lower bowel soft, fecal pellet poorly formed.	Various types of bacteria or other cause of intestinal inflammation.	Prevent stress—wind, rain, poor housing. Do not introduce carrier animals.	Switch diet to Rapid Ade for 1 full week.
Eye infection Baby Adults	In baby rabbits, eyes may stick shut—inflamed eye—may have pus discharge.	Pus under lids in baby rabbits, inflamed eye and eyelids.	Various types of bacteria.	Prevent stress, particularly cold drafts.	Apply specific eye ointment or antibiotic ointment daily.
Fungus infection	Scaly skin over shoulders or along back—hair thin—dandruff.	Excess dandruff and hair thin.	A non-specific fungus.	Prevent contact with affected animal.	Apply 2% lysol solution to affected area every other day for 1 week.
Heat stroke	Panting—mouth open—quiet.	Muscle tissue appears parboiled.	Excessive exposure to direct rays of sun. Lack of adequate ventilation.	Prevent direct exposure to sun or to poorly ventilated quarters.	Submerge in cold water—place in shaded area with adequate ventilation.

Ketosis	Occurs just before or just after kindling, listless, loss of appetite, diarrhea.	Liver large and light colored. Excessive fat in abdomen.	Overfatness—lack of exercise. Reduced feed intake, large litter.	Don't overfeed junior does—encourage exercise — provide palatable feed at kindling.	Prevent overfatness by limiting the feed to 4 to 6 oz. daily of Breeder Paks to Jr. does.
Mastitis— blue breast	Swollen milk gland—tender, may be dark colored—may abscess.	Caked mammary gland—surrounding tissues inflamed.	Bacterial infection. Mechanical injury to mammary gland.	Prevent injury to mammary glands on edge of nest box. Clean and disinfect hutch.	Thoroughly disinfect nest box and hutch. Be sure nails or wire ends are not present on top edge of nest box.
Malocclusion or Buck Teeth	Difficulty in eating, wet about mouth— thin.	Lower teeth protrude— buck teeth— upper teeth long, curve into mouth.	Inherited defect—must be carried by both parents to show up.	Breed from malocclusion free parent stock.	Clip long teeth with sharp wire cutter.
Mucoid Enteritis	Most common at 5 to 8 weeks —excess thirst —pot bellied— diarrhea, feces watery or jelly-like.	Stomach full of water—intestines large— contain jelly like material.	Cause unknown.	Do not introduce carrier stock. Reduce stresses.	Do not introduce rabbits from affected herd. Keep hutches and nest boxes clean.

Pasteurellosis—Hemorrhagic septicemia	Most common in fryers, listless, pot bellied, diarrhea, rapid breathing.	Pneumonia with abscesses in lungs—in does, may have nasal discharge or excess liquid in abdominal cavity in fryers.	Specific bacterial infection, coupled with stress factors.	Don't introduce carrier stock—avoid stress where possible.	Feed Rapid Ade to affected stock and call veterinarian.
Pneumonia	Most common in does, rapid breathing, nasal discharge, head held high.	Abscesses in lungs or solidified areas in lungs.	Bacterial or virus infection, associated with stress factors.	Avoid stress and use good sanitation.	Feed Rapid Ade for 1 week and call veterinarian.
Ringworm	Loss of hair around face, ears, over body; skin inflamed in rings. Do not confuse with hair pulling.	Circular areas of loss of hair, scaly with red inflamed skin.	A specific fungus.	Do not introduce contaminated animal.	Disinfect hutch, then dip all affected rabbits in lime sulphur dip.
Rickets	Occurs only in dark rabbitry. Fore or hind legs crooked. Spraddle legged.	Front or rear legs crooked. Ribs beaded, bones fragile.	Calcium, phosphorus or vitamin D deficiency. No access to sunlight.	Feed a balanced ration and supply direct sunshine.	Supply ample calcium, phosphorus and vitamin D as supplied in Albers Rabbit feed.

Sore hocks	Hunched up or lies stretched out. Pain on walking. Thin.	Scabs usually on bottom of hind feet, may be on front also.	Injury followed by infection of sole of foot. Injury from floor with infections. Insufficient floor support.	Select for thick foot pads. Avoid sharp protruding objects, wire or nails in floor. Avoid wet litter or manure accumulation in pen.	Destroy seriously affected animals. Mildly affected, clean foot with soap and water. Apply saturated solution of Bluestone once weekly. Supply a soft bedding.
Slobbers	Wet about face. Do not confuse with malocclusion. Face may show swelling.	Swollen cheek may contain pus. Intestines lack tone, liquid content.	Excessive feeding of green feed. Indigestion. Abscessed molar teeth.	Do not feed excessive greens.	Cut back on green feed. Extract abscessed tooth. Feed Rapid Ade.
Vent disease	Blisters or dark scabs on external genitals, parts swollen.	Usually no internal lesions.	Urine burn, hot metal floor burn or infection by a spirochete.	Do not allow manure or moisture to accumulate in pens. Do not introduce affected or carrier animals.	Clean off scabs and apply antibiotic ointment or powder and feed Rapid Ade for 7 days.

Courtesy of Albers Milling Company

Feed Companies That Supply Free Material

The following feed companies have materials which they will send the beginner without cost.

A letter to any one of these companies will bring you a list of the various materials available. Some companies have considerable information available, while others have only small booklets. The beginner can learn from them all.

1. Albers Milling Company
   Suite 204, 800 West 47th Street
   Kansas City, Missouri 64112

2. Jim Dandy Company
   1003 North 17th
   Birmingham, Alabama 35203

3. Wayne Rabbit Ration
   Allied Mills, Inc.
   Chicago, Illinois 60609

4. Master Mix
   Central Soya Feed Division
   Fort Wayne, Indiana 46802

5. Red Rose Feed
   John W. Eshelman & Sons
   Lancaster, Pennsylvania 15904

6. Jazz Rabbit Feed
   Cosby-Hodges Milling Company
   Birmingham, Alabama 35203

7. Security Mills
   Knoxville, Tennessee 37901

8. Ralston Purina
   835 South 8th Street
   Saint Louis, Missouri 63102

9. FRM Feed
   Flint River Mills, Inc.
   Tallahassee, Florida 32302

Specialty Clubs

The following rabbit specialty clubs welcome your inquiries and membership. Not only do they provide a quantity of printed material, give advice on specific questions, and publish monthly and semimonthly bulletins, but their members are an excellent source of good breeding stock.

1. National Federation of Flemish Giant
   Rabbit Breeders
   Herb Anthony, Sec.
   746 Garfield Avenue, Newark, Ohio 43055

2. American Federation New Zealand Rabbit
   Breeders

Gordon Fry, Sec.
1206 North 13th St., Arkansas City, Kansas 67005

3. Himalayan Rabbit Club
    Francis P. Riffle, Sec.
    3051 Diamond N.E., Box 4, Middlebranch, Ohio 44652

4. The American Checkered Giant Rabbit Club, Inc.
    Eugene Shultz, Sec.
    502 First National Bank Bldg., Alton, Illinois 62002

5. Rex Rabbit Club
    Mrs. Mary Battista, Sec.
    S-M Farm, Neshanic Station, New Jersey 08853

6. American Polish Rabbit Club
    F. R. Hobias, Sec.
    RFD 3, Box 102, Nazareth, Pennsylvania 18064

7. Beveren Rabbit Club
    Luella M. Mackin, Sec.
    RR 2, Box 46 B, Holden, Missouri 64040

8. National Belgian Hare Club of America

Mrs. June Dutton, Sec.
Route 1, Box 167, South Elgin, Illinois
  60177

9. California Rabbit Speciality Club
   Porter Powers, Sec.
   2040 Temple Hills Drive, Laguna Beach,
     California 92651

10. National Angora Rabbit Breeders Club
    Mrs. Kay Martin, Sec.
    Route 1, Monroe, Indiana 46772

11. Giant Chinchilla Rabbit Association
    Mel Behrens, Sec.
    Box 148, Pearl River, New York 10965

12. Silver Marten Rabbit Club
    H. H. Latham, Sec.
    1421 N.W. 94th Street, Oklahoma City,
      Oklahoma 73114

13. Champagne d'Argent Federation
    Oren R. Reynolds, Sec.
    RR 3, Decatur, Illinois 62526

14. Palomino Rabbit Co-Breeders Association
    Mrs. Dorothy NewPort, Pres.
    2401 Wilson Avenue, S.W., Cedar Rapids,
      Iowa 52404

15. American Chinchilla Rabbit Breeders
    Association
    Robert J. Cebhart, Sec.
    2105 Covington Road, Fort Wayne, Indiana
    46804

Slaughterhouses

Before shipping or delivering rabbit fryers, contact the slaughterhouse and ask about demand, weight required, price being paid, and whether they are in the market for additional suppliers. There are other slaughterhouses throughout the United States that are just as reputable as the following; either their names and addresses were not available when this book was being written or they didn't wish to be listed.

If you do not find a slaughterhouse listed for your area, contact your county agriculture agent or your state department of agriculture. There are many processors who will take a few rabbits regularly but who do not wish to advertise publicly.

1. Teamom Road Farms
   Teamom Road, Box 223X
   Griffin, Georgia 30223

2. Northwest Florida Rabbit Processing Plant
   Box 157A
   Caryville, Florida 32427

3. Pine Crest Rabbitries
   Route 2, Box 35
   Franklinton, Louisiana 70122

4. Rainbow Rabbit Farm
   Old Washington, Ohio 43768

5. Bayou Rabbitry
   Route 1, Box 218
   Plaquemine, Louisiana 70768

6. Alton M. George
   214 W. Vinegard Road
   Griffin, Georgia 30223

7. Mar-Rene Rabbitry and Processing Plant
   U.S. Hwy 41 South
   Brooksville, Florida 33512

8. Gene's Rabbit Ranch
   Route 1, Box 168-C
   Tolleson, Arizona 85353

9. Joseph Laura, Jr.
   RFD 3
   North Middleboro, Massachusetts 02346

10. Happy Chick Farm-Rabbitry
    Route 3, Box 315, Rivers Rd.
    Gulfport, Mississippi 39501

11. H and S Rabbit Processors, Inc.
    Springhill Rd., Route 6, Box 236-A
    Paris, Tennessee 38242

12. Circle G Rabbitry
    70-A Bonanno Court
    Methven, Massachusetts 01844

13. Thompson Rabbit Farm
    Route 2, Box 372
    Teistertown, Maryland 21136

14. Wallick's Rabbitry and Processing Plant
    Zephyrhills, Florida 33599

15. The Arrow Rabbit Ranch
    Statesville, North Carolina 28677

16. Fillmore Rabbit Company
    633 South Fillmore St.
    Allentown, Pennsylvania 18103

17. J & M Rabbit Meat Company
    P O Box 6502
    Shreveport, Louisiana 71106

18. Camden Rabbit Processors, Inc.
    P O Box 351
    Camden, Tennessee 38320

19. A and B Poultry and Rabbit Processors
    2816 Teller Street
    Denver, Colorado 80215

20. Don's Rabbit Farm
    RD 1, Fluvanna Townline Rd.
    Jamestown, New York 14701

21. Ross Flower
    7043 9th Avenue
    Rio Linda, California 95673

Bibliography

American Rabbit Breeders Association. *Official Guide Book.* 1968

Commercial Rabbit Raising. Agriculture Handbook No. 309, United States Department of Agriculture, Washington, D.C. 1960

Florida 4-H Rabbit Manual. University of Florida Agriculture Extension Service, Gainesville, Florida.

Mannell, Paul. *How to Start a Commercial Rabbitry.* Willard, Missouri: Ozark Enterprises, 3rd edition, 1970.

Naether, Carl A. *The Book of the Domestic Rabbit.* New York: David McKay, 1967.

Templeton, George S. *Domestic Rabbit Production.* Danville, Illinois: Interstate Printers and Publishers, 4th edition, 1968.

Index

A

Index

Index

Index

Index

Watering equip. (con't)
  cleaning of, 75–76
  coffee cans as, 45
  crocks as, 45
Watering system,
    automatic, 45–49
Weaning, 107–8
Worm beds, 78,
    163–64

Y

Young
  care of, 99–101
  death of, 102–3
  determining sex of,
    105–6
  embryonic
    development of,
    89
  fostering of, 104–5
  holding of, 107
  nursing of, 97–98
  orphaned, 104
  and predators,
    103–4
  undeveloped,
    99–100
  See also Breeding;
    Kindling; Litters